The Star-Spangled Spangled Retirement Dream

Also by James Gollin

PAY NOW, DIE LATER
WORLDLY GOODS
THE PHILOMEL FOUNDATION

The Star Spangled Retirement Dream

JAMES GOLLIN

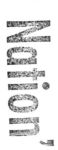

CHARLES SCRIBNER'S SONS • NEW YORK

To the memory of
my father

Copyright © 1981 James Gollin

Library of Congress Cataloging in Publication Data

Gollin, James.
    The star spangled retirement dream.

    Includes bibliographical references and index.
        1. Old age pensions—United States. 2. Social
security—United States. 3. Retirement—United
States.   I. Title.
HD7124.G64   332.024′01   81-4717
ISBN 0-684-16866-9   AACR2

1 3 5 7 9 11 13 15 17 19 Y/C 20 18 16 14 12 10 8 6 4 2

Printed in the United States of America

Contents

PART THREE
How to Make the System Work for You

Introduction
and Acknowledgments

Rather than be a burden to his people, the Kalahari bushman too old to work simply lies down in the shade of a thorn tree and wills himself to die. Similarly, at least according to legend, the Eskimo tribesman who outlives his working years will be handed a single chocolate bar and set adrift on an ice floe to await the end. Societies on the edge of survival can ill afford to be kind and generous to those who can no longer produce. In most of the world's languages, there is no word meaning "retirement."

Thanks to the energy crisis, it may be that all of us in the United States, young *and* old, are about to board the ice floe. Yet even today, as threatened economically as this country may be, few Americans would want to reverse the social processes that, over centuries, have led us first to yearn for an old age free from want and free from toil, then to devote brilliant talent and enormous resources to make the wish come true. We claim to be—in material terms we probably are—the most successful society in history. We pride ourselves on being a humane society. Being both rich and generous has shaped our attitudes and conditioned our

I

reflexes toward retirement. We genuinely do want others, our elders, to be able to retire in comfort. And when our turn comes, we want the same for ourselves.

What exactly do we have in mind?

A soft-spoken, fifty-year-old gentleman named A. Haeworth Robertson expresses our expectations to perfection. Indeed, if anyone can claim to speak with authority on the issue of retirement, he can. Robertson, an actuary, is one of the country's most respected pension administrators. Until 1978, when he joined a private consulting firm, he was chief actuary of the federal Social Security Administration. In Robertson's words:

> Many Americans believe that if they work until about age 60 or 65, they will then be able to live the balance of their lives in carefree and leisurely retirement, occupying themselves with hobbies, sports, and travel—activities for which they had neither the time nor the money in their earlier years. . . . Most people . . . after a few years of nourishing such wants and hopes begin to believe that [this] *should* happen—that they are *entitled* to a leisurely retirement.[1]

This set of beliefs, and the accompanying strong sense of entitlement, Robertson tags "the Great American Retirement Dream."

Were it not for the dream, there would be no reality: no private pension plans enrolling nearly 50 million Americans, no Social Security System to overlap the private plans and gather in more than 150 million members. Without the dream, we would not be spending a startling $50 billion and more *every year* to pay for these programs, or be willing to support within our borders a whole separate nation, at least 20 million strong, of the retired.

And yet, because of the dream, we pay far less attention than we should to the reality. We overlook the millions of people who don't have private pension plans, and the biases and inadequacies built into the existing retirement system. We ignore the uncertainty that underlies retirement planning and the jerry-built character of retirement financing.

Although retirement is one of our very biggest and costliest national endeavors,* Americans everywhere—in the executive suite,

---

*It's noteworthy that on our public schools—which the National Education Association proudly terms "the biggest business in the country"—we spend only $30 billion a year, three-fifths of what we spend to finance retirement.

on the shop floor, in business, in government, in the professions—display almost total ignorance of retirement itself and of the questions surrounding it. Even the experts are ill informed and incurious. For example, the origins of formal retirement planning add up to a fascinating and important chapter in American social history. Business-school professors and government and labor officials tend to know this background and to let it shape their thinking. But of the scores of corporate pension planners and administrators I've met, only a very few have understood how the pension movement began or why pensions were ever a social "movement" in the first place.

Worse still, the experts stay locked in their own closets. The actuaries and consultants who design pension plans never sit down with the sociologists and demographers who chart the social consequences of retirement, or with the psychologists and counselors who deal with its impact on the individual. The social scientists have nothing to do with those other experts who manage retirement-fund investment portfolios. The accountants and the actuaries eye each other warily and seldom address one another except in emergencies.

If the experts seek to know little beyond their own specialties, the lay public knows nothing at all about the experts. But we should be aware that as company-sponsored retirement plans have grown more and more important, an entire industry has quietly come into being to help our employers help *us* retire. For a small company, capable help is not easy to find. But for IBM or the United Auto Workers or the City of Los Angeles, or for any other large-scale employer, things are different. Battalions of lawyers, actuaries, management specialists, investment experts, and even, in this age of communication, writers and artists are eager to go to work on *their* retirement-planning problems. Even if your company is much smaller than IBM, hundreds of retirement-planning firms will scramble to serve it—and some of the strongest, decorously eschewing publicity, scramble just as hard after power and influence in Washington. At stake for them is control over the nation's pension structure—plus, of course, a larger share of the tens of millions of dollars' worth of commissions and fees thrown off by private retirement plans each year.

Because the things the experts do (and don't do) affect most of us only indirectly, it's not surprising that few of us know even the names of the key firms in the retirement-planning business. Much more surprising—and disturbing—is how little attention we pay to our retirement plans themselves. Indeed, there's a good deal of truth in one claim the retirement-planning firms make. We can pick the claim off the sales flip chart of a small but aggressive Westchester County, New York, concern, Compensation Programs, Incorporated.

> The average employee knows the latest jokes, the latest ball scores, all the gossip. But he DOESN'T KNOW THE SCORE on the employee benefits that YOU, Mr. Employer, are providing.

It's not a bad sales pitch. The average employee *doesn't* "know the score." When it comes to his retirement plan, he doesn't even know what kind of game is being played.

For millions of Americans, what's true of company-sponsored benefits is even more true of Social Security. Once more, Haeworth Robertson goes to the heart of the problem. "The average individual," he says, "does not know what Social Security is really all about. He does not know what to expect from Social Security."[2] Exactly. And he certainly has no idea at all of how the Social Security Administration, which sends a check each month to one out of every five Americans, is set up and governed.

To go on multiplying examples would be easy, but by now we should be willing to admit that on the general subject of retirement there is a large gap, a kind of intellectual black hole, between what we do know and what we should know. Part of the reason for the gap, undoubtedly, is that we don't want to know. Thinking about retirement means thinking about growing old, getting poorer, feeling unneeded, facing the deaths of those we love, facing death ourselves . . . and who wants to have to think about such things?

The trouble is, *the way we handle retirement in the United States today cannot possibly meet our needs, much less satisfy our expectations.* True, some of the reasons for this falling short are benign. Who would want to turn the clock back to 1940, when the male American had a life expectancy of 60.8 years—even though the 11 percent increase in average longevity since 1940 has added immeasurably to the cost of supporting the retired?

But other reasons are frightening. The most disturbing problem of all is inflation. On the one hand, inflation is eating away at the pensions and savings of millions of those who have already retired. For a horrifying example of what this can mean, take the case of ninety-one-year-old Mattie Schultz. In July 1979, Mrs. Schultz was arrested and jailed in San Antonio, Texas, on charges of shoplifting fifteen dollars' worth of ham, sausages, and butter from a grocery store. Embarrassed by the subsequent publicity, the store dropped the charge. According to the *New York Times* (July 30, 1979), Mrs. Schultz had to steal the food to "keep from starving" on her $233-a-month income from veterans' benefits and Social Security. When she was caught, Mrs. Schultz (who had often rejected welfare aid) said pathetically that she wanted God "to close my eyes."

On the other hand, the fear of inflation spurs labor leaders to demand higher and higher pension benefits. Passed on to consumers, the cost of such increases—ironically—helps feed the very inflation the increases are intended to offset. Meanwhile, corporations are having trouble with their pension funds. Trying to hold down their contributions, corporations press their actuaries to revise the assumptions on which contributions are based. Trying to increase assets, they demand better and better performance—sometimes at the expense of caution—on the part of their investment advisors. Even so, some commentators are saying that corporation pension obligations are dangerously high in relation to the funds available to cover them. Thus, in November 1977, A. F. Ehrbar outraged the actuarial profession by stating in a *Fortune* story that the difference might be as great as "several hundred *billion* dollars" [emphasis added] and that "the shareholders better watch out."[3]

Barring socioeconomic chaos, corporate pension funds are unlikely to run out of money. Neither are many of us likely to be picked up at ninety-one for shoplifting. But the fact does remain that we can no longer afford to stay ignorant about this knotty subject, to go on placidly dreaming the Great American Retirement Dream, which in brief is the central thesis of this book. To dispel the dreaminess, to bridge the gap of unknowing is the purpose of the chapters that follow.

Retirement is a big, sprawling topic. To deal with it properly, these chapters must range widely. Much of what's wrong (and right) with our current retirement practice is bound up with retirement financing and, specifically, with the plans through which money for retirement is gathered and spent. So, in Part One, we'll examine these plans, public and private, and appraise the planners.

At this point, perhaps a word of reassurance is in order. Retirement planning is a technical subject, like plumbing. Its various aspects enlist the skills of professionals in law, mathematics, and other specialties. Predictably, these insiders communicate with one another in a jargon that to outsiders is both boring and incomprehensible. Part of what this section will do is to translate "pensionese" into English, explain technical terms, and set forth key ideas in plain language.

Woven in with the money issues are issues of social policy. For instance: When should people retire? Should everyone—male and female, executive and laborer, civil servant and soldier—be made to retire at the same age? How much of your income as an active employee will be enough for you to retire on? Is there any sound way to lessen the effect of inflation on the retired? And then, broadening the focus even further: Should retirement mean giving up work entirely? What antidote is there for the "little death" of leaving the job and the workplace behind? Part Two will take up these issues and introduce you to the people who are trying to resolve them.

If we truly are asleep and dreaming, our lullabies are soothing words and phrases. Take the term *retirement plan* itself. It has such a nice, reassuring ring, seeming to imply that you yourself have made a plan for those halcyon years after you retire. Even if you've done no such thing—and you probably haven't—the term suggests, comfortingly, that your company has made one for you. Well, it has and it hasn't. In all of that employee literature you've stuffed away in your desk drawer and vowed you'd read carefully someday, there's a lurking ambiguity. *Retirement plan* refers not to *your* plan but to the company's. The plan does promise to pay you some money. But nowhere does it say anything about what you should do with yourself once you retire. It's simply the smoothest, least expensive way the company can find to ease you out and pension you off when the time is ripe.

In the same vein, reflect on what the federal government means by *Social Security*. Which troubadour of the Roosevelt era coined this wonderful name for something officially christened the "Old-Age, Survivors and Disability Insurance" program? No matter. We may not know, in Haeworth Robertson's phrase, "what Social Security is all about." But we want to believe, even though we worry about its future, that Social Security can deliver just what its name promises: security, underwritten by the greatest planner of them all, Uncle Sam.

Besides your employer and your government, many another enterprise is eager to offer you just the plan for your retirement. "WYNMOOR Village . . . South Florida's most beautiful and AC-TIVE adult community," proclaims the headline of a *New York Times* ad (February 8, 1980). At Wynmoor, you enjoy "lush, tropical landscaping, rolling green fairways . . . vistas of beauty." There's a "new multi-million-dollar Theater and Entertainment Center . . . a showcase of top stars and a gala extravaganza of entertainment." But there's also "full security protection inside and out with the latest sophisticated equipment. . . . Gatehouse guard security and community patrols." To save a place for yourself in this paradise, all you have to do is give Wynmoor Village $45,000 to $75,000.

Some of the planners plan for you to be generous. Take Princeton University's "Bequest Anticipation Plan." Its purpose, says the Princeton brochure, "is to allow you to enjoy your testamentary gift during your lifetime." Huh? No problem: simply leave Princeton in your will "a stated sum of money, in excess of $100,000." Then, while you're still alive enough to be flattered, Princeton will put your name on a professorship.

In contrast, magazines like *The National Geographic* and *Reader's Digest,* heavily read by the old, are full of plans that make thinly veiled appeals to rapacity. "The Franklin Mint Announces Its Newest Series: The Great Paintings of Rembrandt in Medallic Form." The Franklin Mint, of Media, Pennsylvania, has built up a $250-million-a-year business out of the sale of silver-alloy medallions. The Franklin's marketing technique cleverly exploits tradition worship ("Each Medal Beautifully Reproduces a Masterwork"), "rarity" ("When This Limited Edition Is Pressed, The Moulds Will Be Destroyed"), and, not least, the squirrel instinct ("Plan To Acquire the Complete Series . . . Only $15 a Month"). To stimulate the appetite for complete sets of its medals, the mint makes use of an ingenious incentive. At no extra charge, a "subscriber" receives a special display box for his purchases. This little wooden casket holds velvet-lined trays with holes cut in the lining for each medal of the entire set. Month by month, subscribers can fill in the holes until, at last, all of the trays are full and the "collection" is complete. Who, once having subscribed, could bear to cancel his subscription and leave empty spaces in the trays?

Franklin Mint executives identify their best sales prospects as "older men, with time on their hands and some money." Retired military officers must make ideal mint customers. They have the time and the money, and putting together whole sets and series of shiny medals, arranging and rearranging them in their cases, should appeal strongly to the military passion for neatness, order, and display.

When it comes to retirement, it seems that everybody's got a plan for you—except you.

This is the heart of the matter. We owe ourselves a hard look at the answers the actuaries and forecasters and social scientists—not to mention the ad men, the marketing wizards, and all our other peddlers of goods and services—have in store for America the aging. But also, throughout this book and especially in its third and final section, you'll be invited to turn your back on the sweeping questions and the bravura solutions, to forget about how this or that retirement issue affects the whole polity, and to concentrate on how it affects you. The most provocative questions of all are the most personal ones. How will I deal with my own retirement? Have I enough time? Will my approach be a success or a disaster?

This book, its themes, and its ideas have crystallized gradually in my mind. During eight and a half years as a life-insurance agent I learned the rudiments of selling pension plans to small businesses. In the late 1960s, as a writer and editor for Johnson & Higgins, I was involved in the very different game of marketing pensions and pension services to big corporations. Through the 1970s, Johnson & Higgins, William M. Mercer, and other pension consulting firms afforded me free-lance assignments and the chance to stay abreast of what was happening in the field. Much *was* happening. From being a peripheral issue, retirement planning was moving closer and closer to the center of our social concerns. Having watched the process for years, I think it's time to report.

Many people have helped me make this report. Perhaps the best way to acknowledge the help is to single out, by profession or position, those who were most generous with their time and aid.

Actuaries

Barnet N. Berin, Kenneth K. Keene, Norman R. Minor, Jeff Radov, and Shepard A. Sheinkman. For explaining and exemplifying to this nonactuary what an actuary should be, I owe special gratitude to the late Clark T. Foster. Linda Delgadillo, communications director of the Society of Actuaries, Chicago, Illinois, supplied the essential statistics and many shrewd insights as well.

Lawyers

Lloyd S. Kaye's encyclopedic knowledge of benefit-plan law and practice makes him a master in the field. His mordant wit makes him the most entertaining of instructors. Richard Fay was an expert guide through the political thickets of federal pension reform.

Financial Specialists

Frank W. Burr, Jane C. Mack, Philip F. Metcalf, John M. Morris, and Stephen Rogers were all patient and candid beyond the call of duty. All are in the top ranks of their respective fields.

Government Officials

I am deeply indebted to Ms. Shelley Lapkoff of the President's Commission on Pension Policy, Washington, D.C., and to other members of the commission's remarkable staff, including in particular Ms. Leigh McDermott of the press office and Ms. Carol Thompson, the librarian.

Dennis Snook and Duke Wilson of the Study Group for Universal Social Security went out of their way to provoke thought and render assistance.

William C. Russell (Department of Labor) and Charles Bryson (Securities and Exchange Commission) answered my queries and suggested other people to consult about issues. James Brown (Social Security Administration) was similarly helpful to a neophyte in Washington research. Len Lenoci (Pension Benefit Guaranty

Corporation) described in detail the background of his agency.

On Capitol Hill, Russell J. Mueller (Pension Task Force, House Committee on Education and Labor) took pains to explain public-sector pension problems.

In nonofficial Washington, I owe thanks to Miss Martha C. Derthick, director of governmental studies at the Brookings Institution, for her help, and to the institution itself for permission to quote from Miss Derthick's *Policymaking for Social Security.* * In addition, I wish to thank Dr. Edmund Fitzpatrick of the National Council on the Aging and Betty Benkala of the statistical services staff of the American Council of Life Insurance. Robert W. Waldron, manager of the council's press office in New York, displayed interest in the book and commendable restraint toward its author, whom he characterized amiably as a "long-term thorn in our side."

To the directors and staffs of the library of the College of Insurance, New York, and of the Sterling Memorial Library, Yale University, my thanks for access to their shelves and stacks.

Nearer at hand, I wish to express my gratitude to Ruth Ann Waite, formerly of Paul R. Reynolds, Inc., my agent at the outset of this project. Her interest and support were good deeds in a naughty world. Just as exceptional is the kindness and resourcefulness of my present agent, William C. Reiss of the Reynolds firm. At Charles Scribner's Sons, Jacek Galazka has been a fatherly chief editor. Susanne Kirk, who inherited this book and its author when *The Star-Spangled Retirement Dream* still *was* a dream, has borne patiently and understandingly the burden of being my working editor.

Others too have talked with me about retirement and retirement issues. Some have supplied information. Some have argued a particular point of view. To all not named above, as to those whose names do appear, my thanks. The flaws and failings of this book, needless to add, are not yours, but mine alone.

My two sons, Timothy and Douglas, are by now hardened to having an author for a father. They could not have been more patient, more indulgent, or more exacting in matters of grammar and syntax. Nor could my wife, Jane Gollin, without whose encouragement and love I could write nothing at all.

PART ONE

★

The System

★ 1 ★

Private Pensions:
Darling, You Are Growing Old

On the first day of your present job, the last thing on your mind was retiring from it. Nor, to recruit you, did your employer put an ad in the help-wanted columns that read: "Engineer, exp'd. To $20k. Retire at 65 on 60% pension" or, "Mgr. sales & serv, sal $18,000 plus subsidized early retirement." Things just don't happen this way. Nevertheless, sometime early in your employment, you probably did ask about the retirement plan. You may have talked to your boss, or to the people in Personnel. You may have attended a lecture on the subject as part of the company's orientation program. If you were brought aboard at a high enough level, you may even have received a personal briefing on the plan from the official in charge of it.

In any event, although retirement itself seemed as far off as Alpha Centauri II, it was perfectly natural to check out the retirement plan. One of the reasons you're at work, after all, is for the security the plan represents. Besides, you were curious to see how this plan stacked up against the one old Tightwad & Company finally put in just before you quit to come here.

The chances are, too, that when you asked, you received a pleasantly reassuring answer—"Oh, we've got a *very* good plan here"—plus a sheaf of printed material that "explains" the plan. Later, if you work for a large company, the folks in Personnel or Employee Benefits will be sending you a "personalized statement" written by a computer. This, if you can decipher it, is meant to keep you up to date on your retirement-plan standing and keep you mindful of the company's generosity in offering the plan. Why not? What's wrong with wanting you to know that for every dollar the company puts into your salary it puts another twenty cents (on the average) into your retirement account?

There's nothing wrong. Yet, from your point of view, a couple of things are less than right. The brochures that supposedly explain your retirement benefits may not explain them very clearly. And the way the explanation is presented will tend to obscure some important truths. One is that your company isn't running its retirement plan solely out of kindness or compassion for its employees. On the contrary, it has hardheaded business reasons for setting up its plan—reasons that have nothing to do with humanitarianism.

Another truth, with which we'll be dealing in due course, is that your company's plan, as attactive as the literature may make it appear, almost certainly won't provide enough money for you to retire on.

Why *do* companies operate retirement plans? The answer is *money.* Companies are in business to make money, and to make money they need efficient, productive employees. As employees gain experience, their productivity increases, and so does their compensation. But beyond a certain age, the loss of physical strength and stamina and the decline in alertness and the ability to concentrate produce a slackening of efficiency and productivity. Not all the experience in the world—so goes the theory—can make good these losses. At the same time, compensation has reached a peak. The employer is thus in the position of having to shell out top dollar for deteriorating performance.

At this point, the employer has two choices. He can continue to employ the decreasingly productive oldster and hope the poor devil will quit (or die) before too long. If the employer makes this his policy, he'll soon have a company full of expensive, increasingly ineffectual employees. In a competitive world, this is not the sort of labor force most employers feel they need.

The more prudent choice, of course, is to get rid of the overage employee. This can be done by caprice ("Good old Ed. Heads, he stays. Tails, he goes.") or by rule ("Sorry, Ed, but around here it's sixty-five and out."). But either way, the falling axe is as apt to damage the wielder as the victim. If the employer has no set cutoff date, he takes on himself the tricky business of deciding in each case when it's time to drag the individual to the scaffold—plus the equally delicate task of explaining to good old Ed, whose turn has come at sixty-five, why good old Charley, who's also sixty-five, gets to stay on. It's fairer and more practical to let employees know in advance when they'll have to go. But if an employer forewarns people that they'll be leaving at sixty or sixty-five, the chances are strong that some of them won't feel like working *too* hard at fifty or fifty-five—or even like staying around at all.

For this set of problems, a plan that turns dismissal for old age into honorable, paid retirement is truly a brilliant solution. Such a plan gives the employer a velvet glove to slip over the iron hand of enforced termination. It offers a way to reward loyalty and to encourage productivity right up to the last hour on the job. It substitutes a known benefit for any other claim an employee may have—or may feel he has—against his former employer. Best of all, while a retirement plan does cost money, it costs less than carrying the incompetent elderly on the payroll. And the costs can be estimated in advance and spread out over long periods of time.

Needless to say, this rationale is not in the mind of the corporate treasurer every time he makes an adjustment in the retirement plan. Or in that of the union bargainer as he tries for another ten-dollar-a-month pension increase. These pragmatists take retirement plans for granted as part of the personnel and labor-relations apparatus. But whatever they do, it's important for you to remember that your company's plan, useful though it may be, wasn't designed with *you* in mind.

For a plan of any size, the designer will almost certainly be a consulting actuary. In chapter 3, we'll meet some of these specialists in applied mathematics. We'll learn how their firms—carrying such names as William M. Mercer, Incorporated; Kwasha, Lipton & Company; George S. Buck & Company; and the Wyatt Company—have come to dominate the retirement-planning business. Here, it's enough to note that these firms, and a handful of others like them, do most of the studies and make most of the recommendations that major employers follow.

When he goes to work on a retirement plan, the actuary starts with the client's labor force. His raw material is the data gleaned from the personnel files on employee ages, earnings, service, and dependents. Even in the era of the computer, this information is often hard to put together—and harder to hone into accuracy. Also important are the past results—the "experience," actuaries say—of the existing plan, if one in fact exists. Then, too, the actuary will take into account such broader concerns as the type of industry in question, the retirement plans of the client's competitors, and the cash-flow patterns of the client itself.

One of the first decisions the actuary will have to make is which type of plan to recommend. He has two types to choose from: defined-benefit and defined-contribution plans. In a defined-benefit plan, the known factor is what the employees themselves will receive at retirement. Year by year, the outlay to finance this type of plan will vary. In contrast, the given of a defined-contribution plan is the amount to go into the plan each year; the variables are the benefits. Pension plans, by definition, are defined-benefit plans. Profit-sharing and savings, or "thrift," plans are defined-contribution plans. Neither type is necessarily better than the other, each one being chosen for a specific purpose. But in terms of importance, most employers rank pensions higher. According to a recent *Fortune* survey, almost every one of the "*Fortune* 1000" largest industrial corporations provides pension benefits, but only about 32 percent offer profit-sharing or thrift plans.[1]

Whether he's developing a new plan or revising an old one, the actuary will deal with the same set of key provisions. These are (1) eligibility (who gets into the plan, and how); (2) the formula (how the retirement income is figured);* (3) vesting (when the people in the plan gain legal rights to their benefits); (4) what forms the benefits will take; and (5) how and when the benefits are paid. Viewed dispassionately, these fundamentals are interesting. The way they're put together can be revealing. Accordingly, it's well worth the effort to take up each of them in turn.

---

* In the case of defined-contribution plans, how contributions are determined.

ELIGIBILITY

Before 1974, when Congress passed the law known as ERISA,* your employer could make it hard to get into the retirement plan. You might have had to meet stiff age, earnings, and service requirements—for example, to have been at least twenty-five, or even thirty, *and* to have worked for the company at least five years, *and* to be earning more than, say, $500 a month.

A big company would justify such stringency on grounds of cost. Its actuary would run studies to show that the turnover rate was highest among its youngest, newest, and lowest-paid employees. Before the Internal Revenue Service (which, until ERISA, sat in sole judgment on retirement plans), the company would argue that (a) it cost a lot of money to sign up someone in the retirement plan; (b) of the new, young workers, few (if any) would stay around long enough to collect benefits; *ergo* (c) it was wasteful to spend the money to sign them up and (d) fair to exclude them altogether.

Some very big organizations do hire droves of young, low-paid employees and let them come and go like so many little mice. Often, the pay is low because the recipient works part time. Especially in retail businesses like department stores and supermarkets, there's some substance to the cost argument for keeping the casual employee—"the Christmas help"—out of the retirement plan.

But many other companies in other industries have used the same argument without the same need and with a different purpose. Their managements believed that a retirement plan was not something to which every youngster was entitled. Rather, it was a reward for hard work and loyal service, and one that only seasoned employees had earned.

Far more self-serving were the motives behind the eligibility provisions of tens of thousands of retirement plans set up by small corporations. Many such firms, of course, are no more than individual proprietorships or partnerships, run by their owners and perhaps a few clerks or salespeople. But their owners found out that if they incorporated, they could list themselves, along with

---

* For *E*mployee *R*etirement *I*ncome *S*ecurity *A*ct. We'll be encountering ERISA repeatedly throughout this book. For its background and provisions, see chapter 7.

their underlings, as employees. Then they could put in a plan, buy themselves employee retirement benefits, and *deduct the cost from their business income.* "Jeez!" I once heard a hardware wholesaler exclaim when these verities were set before him. "It's just like being General Motors!"

The problem was to make sure—staying within the IRS regulations—that most of the money going into the plan, and preferably every penny, was put in for the owners, not for those who only worked in the place. This could be a challenge. But an agile pension draftsman with a good sense of what the IRS would and would not reject as "discriminatory" under Section 413.1(a) of the Tax Code could generally come up with an answer that eliminated everybody *but* the owners.

Until ERISA, most companies wrote one other eligibility rule into their retirement plans. This one barred from the plan anybody *older* than a given age, usually fifty-five. The rationale was that it cost too much money to buy retirement benefits for someone already so near retirement. (The reason will be clear after our look, in chapter 3, at retirement-plan funding.) Indeed, if you were lucky enough to catch on with a big corporation when you were over fifty-five, you used to have to sign a form waiving any right to retirement benefits.

ERISA put an end to the "they're either too young or too old" attitude of so many employers. Even before 1974, a number of major companies were liberalizing their eligibility rules. Some simply saw the handwriting on the wall. Union pressure influenced others. But more a factor in the decision than anything else was the advent of the computer, which made nonsense of the argument, for most employers, that it was too expensive to keep tabs on the young and the restless. Once service and earnings records are in the computer, it costs next to nothing to update them. Normal turnover will probably shake out most of the added "eligibles" anyway. So why not allow new, young employees into the retirement plan?

Now, employers must open their plans to all employees who have reached twenty-five and have been with the company for a year. A year equals 1,000 hours of work, a definition that makes a great many part-timers eligible to join a company plan. Employers are still allowed to exclude older employees, but as a rule, only those who are older than sixty when they're hired are being kept out of the plans.

THE FORMULA

In a pension plan, the retirement benefit will almost always be some form of annuity. An annuity is an income that starts when you retire and continues for at least the rest of your life.*

How much of an income?

Clearly, the company can't pick the figure out of a hat the day before your retirement dinner. Nor can the company play favorites. Say you're in line for a pension of $800 a month. What happens when your colleague down the hall in Marketing—he's your age, he makes exactly what you make, and he works about half as hard—lets slip that he's going to be retiring on $1,000 a month? To put it mildly, you're not going to be too happy with your employer.

To spare the company such problems, the actuary bases everybody's retirement benefits on a formula. This will link the benefits to each employee's earnings, years of service, or both. Because it spells out in detail the employer's financial obligations to retiring employees, the formula is the linchpin of the entire plan.

Some pensions have very simple formulas. Among most union members, for example, seniority is what counts. Union people like their pensions to be based entirely on service and the amounts spelled out in terms of the number of dollars of monthly pension awarded per year of service. That way, the more senior you are, the bigger your pension—and never mind what anybody *earns.* Or, in medium-sized and small companies, where turnover is low and salaries remain stable from year to year, the formula even for white-collar employees can be as uncomplicated as: "The retirement benefit shall be 30 percent of the employee's salary at the time of retirement."

But in big companies, a scramble, not stasis, is the norm. People in white collars are constantly campaigning for promotions and transfers and raises. They hop from department to depart-

---

* Profit-sharing plans may also provide for annuity payments to members, but they need not do so.

ment, from division to division, even from country to country. They leave, work somewhere else for a while, then come back.

The senior management that presides over a big white-collar work force—think of Ma Bell or Citicorp or IBM—knows it has to be fair with its well-educated, competitive employees. But within the limits of fairness, it also wants to be able to use the pension as a carrot. This means nailing *your* benefits as tightly as possible to *your* company loyalty and *your* performance. Working both earnings *and* service into the pension formula helps management distinguish precisely between you and the marketing executive down the hall.

Straining after both fairness and individualization can produce some remarkably obscure verbiage in a pension formula. Thus:

> For every year of service prior to April 1, 1972, the employee shall be credited with a retirement benefit equal to 1.75 percent of his annual base salary during the year; and for every year of service subsequent thereto, the employee shall be credited with a retirement benefit equal to 2 percent of his annual base salary . . .

While this formula could certainly stand translation out of its native "legalese" into English, it's not as complicated as it looks. In fact, a brief analysis of it will shed light on how most plan formulas work. First, note that the formula takes into account two periods of employee service: a period before April Fools' Day, 1972, and a period after that date. For the first period, the one before the plan was installed (or the present formula adopted), the employee's benefits are computed on one basis. For service *after* the start-up of the plan or formula, the benefits are figured a bit differently.

To compute the benefits for the period of past service,* you need know only (a) the number of years between the time the employee joined the plan and April 1, 1972, and (b) the employee's earnings for each of these years. For instance, suppose someone

---

* In pension jargon, the term *past service* is extremely important. Now is a good time to underscore that "past service" *always* refers to service before a plan or formula took effect. Thus, an actuary writing in 1980 about the past service of an employee in a plan that was begun in 1972 is referring to service before 1972, not service before 1980. Retirement plans have pasts and futures of their own.

joined on April 1, 1967, was then earning $14,000 a year, and in each of the four subsequent years was given a thousand-dollar raise. A couple of minutes with a calculator is all it takes to multiply each year's salary by 1.75 percent and add up the five answers. The total is $1,400. When the employee ultimately begins to draw his retirement income, $1,400 of the yearly total will be the portion generated by the five years of past service.

Figuring the benefits for service *after* April 1, 1972, is done in exactly the same fashion, except that each year's benefit is 2 percent of the salary for the year, not 1.75 percent. Finding the total benefit, of course, must wait until the employee actually retires. Only then can his pay for his last year be known, the 2 percent benefit computed, and this sum added to all the others.

The main thing to note about this formula, and most others used in large plans, is that it operates cumulatively. It credits the employee with a small benefit, a kind of mini-annuity, for each year of service. Add up all the credits and you have the total pension. Arithmetically, there's another way to arrive at the same result: Work out the *average* earnings figures for the two periods of service, past and future, multiply these by the benefit percentages, and multiply the answers in turn by the number of years in each period. If you apply this alternative arithmetic to the example above, you find that the average salary for the employee's five years of past service is $16,000. Multiplied by 1.75 percent, this amount produces an average benefit of $280. And $280 times the number of years of past services yields the expected answer, a total past-service benefit of $1,400.

Because the earnings used are those of the employee's entire career, actuaries with the averaging method of figuring benefits in mind would style this formula a *career-average* formula. In some situations, actuaries favor basing benefits not on career-average earnings but on *final averages:* averages of earnings over the last years—usually, the last five years—of employee careers. Typically, salaries rise over working lifetimes and are at their highest during the years immediately before retirement. A final-average formula will therefore produce a much higher pension than would a career-average formula using the same benefit percentages.

Inflation makes a final-average formula seem fairer to the employee, because his pension is clearly related to what he was earning just before retirement. But career-average formulas can be adjusted every few years to compensate for inflation, and their costs are more predictable; the advantage of the final-average formula is more a matter of appearance than of reality. Nevertheless, actuarial battles are waged, and accounts lost and won, over the career-average *versus* final-average issue.

Other questions also preoccupy those who work up pension formulas. Should the formula take any notice of Social Security retirement benefits? Should it be made more generous, the added benefits to be paid for by employee contributions? In the chapters on pension finance and Social Security (chapters 3 and 6), we'll take up both of these important questions.

VESTING

Let's assume that you're forty-five, that you've been with the XYZ company for nine years, and that for eight of these years, you've been a member of the company's pension plan. XYZ has run into hard times. It has to cut back, and you've just learned that the surgery starts with you. As you're cleaning out your desk, you come upon the retirement-plan literature. The discovery spurs you to wonder, *What happens to my retirement benefits?* You call Personnel to find out, and the voice at the other end of the phone makes your day complete by saying, "Sorry. All gone."

You make squawking noises.

Yes, the voice says, you *were* in the plan. Yes, you *did* accumulate eight years' worth of benefits. But because you're leaving so soon, your benefits, well, evaporate. Too bad, but that's the way the plan works.

You hang up. You have just learned—the hard way—what *vesting* means.

Used properly, the term *vesting* means bestowing a legal right on someone. Thus, the day you pay off your auto loan, the bank vests in you the full title to your car. But for some unknown reason, pension planners give the term their own twist. They "vest" you, not your benefits.

Once an employee retires, he obviously must have, and does have, a legal right to his pension benefits. But until he retires, this right is by no means absolute. During the early decades of pension planning, it was unthinkable for employers to concede any rights at all to future retirement income to an employee still at work.

Why, the fellow might quit and go to work for someone else—and still demand a pension from us! It would be giving away the company's money! That an employee who left had *earned* some pension benefits for his services was an idea slow to take hold in the American business community.

But unless the employee was given some protection, an unscrupulous employer could use the pension plan to assure the employee's loyalty and then, a year or six months before his retirement, simply fire him and thus save the cost of the pension. Such incidents occurred often enough to anger labor organizations, congressmen, and Internal Revenue Service pension regulators. So rules were written requiring at least partial vesting of pension rights.

Even then, employers used vesting requirements as they used eligibility requirements; to try to screen out the younger, more restless employees and to treat the pension as a special reward for loyalty. Before any of his pension credits were vested, the employee had to satisfy a combined age-and-service requirement. And the vesting itself might be gradual. Full vesting might not be permitted until the individual was forty-five or fifty and had completed twenty years of service.*

Now, under the ERISA pension law, the employee cannot be made to wait so long for protection of his rights. While several methods are allowable, most employers today are simply vesting full rights in employees who had finished ten years of service, regardless of age.

FORMS OF BENEFITS

On page 19, we noted that in a pension plan the actual retirement benefit is almost always an annuity. It can be, and often is, a "pure annuity," one that begins at an employee's retirement, pays him an income for the rest of his life, and stops when he dies. But most employers offer retiring employees alternatives to the pure annuity. These can be very useful, but employers and actuaries consider them hard to explain. Because they offer something

---

* Note that what is vested is the right to the pension the employee had gained at the time he left the company, not to the pension he would have received if he'd stayed until retirement.

extra, they cost more. And the employee is made to absorb the added cost by accepting a reduced income.

The most frequently offered options add extra guarantees to the basic annuity. These are:

- A guarantee that if the retired employee dies before receiving a given number of pension payments, usually five or ten years' worth, the outstanding payments will be made to the employee's beneficiary
- A guarantee that the employee's surviving spouse will receive a fraction (generally one-half or two-thirds) of the pension for life following the employee's own death
- A guarantee to the employee who retires early of larger monthly benefits until Social Security payments begin, with reduced benefits afterward, to even out total retirement income

To see how the costs of these alternatives compare, take the case of a male employee who retires at sixty-five, is the same age as his wife, and is entitled to a pure annuity income of $10,000 a year. If he chooses the first of the alternatives, and elects a ten-year guarantee, his income drops to $9,100 a year. If he instead decides that he wants half of his own income to be paid to his widow after his death, his income is reduced to $8,670. These are stiff prices to pay for what is, in effect, postretirement life insurance protection. The costliness explains why very few employees make use of any method of settlement other than the pure annuity.

In Part Three, we'll look more closely at these alternatives, and at one other method of pension payout, to see which might be best for you.

RETIREMENT AGE

In June 1977, William M. Mercer, Inc., a large employee-benefit consulting firm, released the results of a survey of 400 senior corporate executives on the subject of mandatory retirement. According to the survey report:

> By 67% to 21%—over 3 to 1—executives say mandatory retirement is necessary to create job openings and advancement opportunities for younger people. . . . [Yet] management does feel—and by a strong 68% to 23% majority—that [mandatory retirement] deprives society of the experience and value of older people.[2]

Later that year, in December, Congress passed a law barring employers from forcing into retirement employees younger than seventy. An exception was made for "managerial and supervisory" employees earning $21,000 or more a year. Such employees can be required to accept retirement at sixty-five.

Meanwhile, during the past six or seven years, some employers have become interested in *lowering* the retirement age to sixty-two, or sixty, or even younger. Their interest is in response to union pension bargaining. The United Auto Workers and the steelworkers have fought hard for the so-called thirty-and-out option, which enables their members to retire on full pension after thirty years of service, regardless of age. And associations and unions of public employees—in particular, policemen, firemen, and sanitation workers—have won the right to full pensions after twenty-five or even twenty years of service.

Executive ambivalence, the congressional action, and the union effort all strongly suggest that American society is perplexed by the question of when people should, in the memorable phrase of British novelist C. P. Snow, "put my 'In' box in my 'Out' box and go home for good."*

In most countries, sixty-five has won acceptance as the age to mark the border between active work and retirement. There's no special reason why sixty-five, and not sixty-four, sixty-three, or sixty—or seventy—should have been chosen. Indeed, when Prince Otto von Bismarck set up the first state-run retirement system, in 1884 in Prussia, he picked seventy as the earliest age at which people could retire. According to Barnet N. Berin, head of pension actuarial services for the Mercer firm, "Age sixty-five was a compromise in the United States between those who wanted sixty and those who supported seventy." Nevertheless, sixty-five is the nearest thing there is to an official normal retirement age. Full Social Security benefits are payable at sixty-five, and it's still recognized as the normal age for retirement in most corporate pension plans.

Most of these plans also provide for retirement at other ages. A typical arrangement allows an employee to retire early, at any time after he's within ten years of his normal retirement date. But

---

* "I shall be able to put my In-tray on top of my Out-tray and go back to something worth doing." (C. P. Snow, *The New Men*. New York: Scribners, 1954.)

if you retire early, you may well have to do so on a reduced pension. On the one hand, you'll have had fewer years of service during which to earn pension credits, and the investment fund for your benefits will have had fewer years in which to grow. On the other hand, you're probably going to be collecting your benefits for longer than the fifteen years or so that are the norm for somebody who retires at sixty-five. To stretch out the lesser sum of money over the greater period of time, the company's actuary will lower the amount of the income.

Retiring after sixty-five, however, is very unlikely to mean a *higher* pension. Although your benefits will certainly cost the company less and less the longer you postpone them, the company will probably point out that your salary is costing it more and more. At least, that's the excuse they'll give you for not stepping up your retirement income.

You may feel about retirement as does George J. Becker, who at sixty-two is president and chief executive of Giddings & Lewis, Inc., a Wisconsin machine-tool manufacturer. The *Wall Street Journal* (September 13, 1977) quoted Becker as saying: "I don't want to work after I'm 65. I'll want to do something, but I don't want to come in here at 7:30 in the morning and work until 6 at night." Or you may side with Ruth Ellen Lindenberg, a social services teacher at Cleveland State University, who said to the *Journal,* "I think the ultimate insult is to be told you are a different person because you are 65." Either way, the chances are excellent that you'll be able to do what earlier generations of employees could not do: choose your own preferred time to retire.

You've had a chance to consider the purposes behind retirement plans. You've seen that their provisions, far from being eternal, immutable, and set in stone, are almost infinitely adjustable. Although retirement plans clearly do benefit employees, you've begun to perceive that they're primarily tools of management, or what Paul Isenman, an economist with the World Bank in Washington, D.C., aptly calls "instruments of social control."

How did these tools originate? When? Who were their earliest users? How does the past history of retirement planning affect today's practices? These are the matters to be scrutinized next.

★ 2 ★

How Pensions Began:
The Origin of the Dream

Throughout history, a secure retirement has been the privilege of the few, and pensions have been the gifts of princes to their favorites. Poets, like advertising copywriters today, have loved to idealize retirement. Take for example Athos, the noblest and most Byronic of Alexandre Dumas's Three Musketeers. In *Le Vicomte de Bragelonne,* the vast sequel to this classic, Dumas portrays Athos in his forties and fifties, in retirement at Blois, content with his modest château, his thirty acres of garden and vineyard, his books, and his beloved young son. The setting is idyllic, a French Arcadia. Or consider the real-life instance of Sir Henry Lee (1533–1610), whose retirement from service to Queen Elizabeth in 1590 was immortalized by John Dowland in a touching song for lute. "My Helmet now," the poet makes the aging champion say, "shall make an hiue for Bees."

But for most of mankind, retirement has been a much uglier reality, a time of physical decay, destitution, and helplessness in the face of illness and death. Pensions were not originally meant to remedy the economic miseries of hordes of the aged. Rather, from the beginning, pensions have been tools of governance, awards to be granted to a select few for extraordinary service to the state.

The Athenians gave pensions to their victorious generals. The veterans of Rome's armies were given pensions in the form of farmland in outlying regions of the empire—hence, Romania. In India and China, high civil functionaries could count on receiving pensions from the royal treasuries. An economic historian can gauge the gradual emergence of the money economy in Europe by following the shift in the system of royal rewards. Thus, William the Conqueror and his successors to the throne of England for five hundred years made land the basis for the rewards (and punishments) they meted out to their servants. In terms of prestige, land long remained paramount. But by Queen Elizabeth's day, monetary prizes, such as reversions* and monopolies, had assumed critical importance. The shrewd Elizabeth saw that gifts of income, unlike gifts of land, could be withheld or withdrawn as readily as they could be given. And, brilliant executive that she was, she knew how to crack the whip. One of the causes of the downfall of the Earl of Essex was the Queen's refusal, in 1598, to renew her favorite's exclusive right (or "monopoly") to collect taxes on imports of sweet wines. "An unruly beast," said Elizabeth, "must be stopped of his provender." The stoppage deprived Essex of most of his revenue. His desperate response to the loss, an act of open rebellion, cost him his head.

In the absence of exact knowledge about human longevity, people could only guess at the true values of the reversions, monopolies, and annuities that were being substituted for interests in land. This made for much discontent. In the middle of the seventeenth century, a series of discoveries began to make longevity understandable in mathematical terms. The keystone of this new theoretical structure was Blaise Pascal's *Treatise on Probability* (1654). Applying Pascal's theories on the odds of dice and playing cards to the odds of life and death soaked up the energies of an

---

* A reversion was the right to take over a government or court post at the death or withdrawal of the incumbent. Because a reversion carried with it an assurance of future income, it had a present cash value. This depended on such factors as the age and health of the incumbent and the estimate by the buyer of how much he could make out of the appointment.

entire generation of mathematicians. In 1661, John Graunt published a remarkable pamphlet entitled *Natural and Political Observations on the Bills of Mortality.* These "bills" were the monthly reports of deaths and their causes. Graunt's scrutiny was in fact the very first exercise in demography. His idea of using survivorship from year to year to measure the rate at which people die was to be the basis of actuarial mathematics.

Others as ingenious as Graunt carried on similar research. Abraham de Moivre was a French mathematician who lived in London and, during most of his career, worked as an oddsmaker for professional gamblers. (Today, we'd style him a "betting commissioner.") De Moivre found time to write a monograph, *Annuities on Lives,* in which he propounded a beautifully simple law of mortality. According to de Moivre, 1 out of every 86 infants born alive would die every year until the last died at the age of $85\frac{1}{2}$.

De Moivre's law turned out to be *too* simple. One of the first to correct it was the celebrated mathematician and astronomer Edmund Halley. The precocious Halley, elected to the Royal Society at twenty-two and at twenty-eight the benefactor and publisher of Isaac Newton, was curious about the mathematics of longevity. On a trip to Germany in 1679, Halley uncovered a highly reliable source of vital statistics in the city registers of Breslau, the capital of Saxony. He used the data to prepare a mortality chart far more accurate than that of de Moivre. Halley's table was published in 1693. De Moivre, to his credit, devoted a great deal of effort to promoting the discoveries of his distinguished junior.

Meanwhile, in 1670–71, a Dutch public servant was quietly studying an administrative problem. To carry on the naval war against England, the States-General of Holland needed money. In this most money-conscious of European nations, it had long been a practice to raise public funds by selling annuities. That is, an individual could turn over a sum of guilders to the government and in exchange be guaranteed an income, either for his own life or for that of some nominee. In effect, the purchaser was betting the state that he (or the nominee) would live long enough to collect more than had been turned over. The government had been offering its annuities to customers of all ages at the rate of nine years' purchase. This meant that if the annuitant lived for nine years, the buyer would break even; if the annuitant lived longer, the buyer could end up very far ahead. The States-General was uneasy about this price structure. Was it asking too little and paying out too much? For answers, the members turned to Jan De Witt, the grand pensionary* of Holland and West Friesland.

De Witt did what John Graunt had done and what Edmund Halley was soon to do: He dug into the actual statistics of the case. From his examination of what had befallen previous annuitants, he drew some disquieting conclusions. For the buyer, a nine-years'-purchase annuity was a tremendous bargain. For the government, it was a disaster. Recent price increases to twelve and fourteen years' purchase were still not large enough. Even at sixteen years' purchase, a government annuity on the life of a young and healthy applicant was an excellent buy. De Witt buttressed his findings with a full set of figures and a mortality table. But even though his report attracted a certain amount of attention and caused the government to raise annuity prices, it was treated as a confidential state document and was buried in the archives. (In fact, De Witt's report went unpublished until 1851.)

For decades after mathematicians had established the framework for sensibly financed state pensions, the rulers of Europe continued to distribute pensions without the least concern for their ultimate cost. In England, Charles II handed out pensions to scores of his friends and to his several mistresses as well. The king's generosity was certainly appropriate. Charles himself was secretly receiving a pension from that supposedly implacable enemy of Britain, Louis XIV of France.

A law dating from the first year of Queen Anne's reign (1702) forbade the Crown to burden its hereditary revenues with pensions lasting longer than the lifetime of the reigning sovereign. But the law applied only to the revenues of England. The early Hanoverians simply turned to their Scottish and Irish estates. George I gave his two German mistresses, Ehrengarde Melusina, Duchess of Kendal, and Charlotte Sophia, Countess of Darlington, Irish pensions with a combined worth of £5,000 a year (about $100,000 in today's money). George II rewarded a mistress, Madame de Walmoden, with an Irish pension of £3,000 a year.

George III reluctantly gave up control of the Crown revenues

* This title, interestingly, had nothing to do with pensions. It was simply the honorific of the chief legal and financial official of the Dutch Republic.

in favor of a "civil list" established by Parliament at the outset of his reign. But by no means did he forego the use of the pension as a political weapon. While the king lived penuriously, he spent money lavishly to gain power over Parliament. Pensions granted "during the king's pleasure" were most often thinly disguised bribes.

The king and his ministers sometimes wielded this weapon with great finesse. For instance, in 1762 they offered a pension of £300 a year to Samuel Johnson, of dictionary fame. The pension was paraded as a recognition of the great man's literary merit—only that and nothing more. Nevertheless, Dr. Johnson hesitated. As staunch a Tory as it was possible to be, he held that the Hanoverian dynasty had gained the throne via usurpation. And in his great *Dictionary of the English Language* (1755), he had composed for the word *pension* one of the most acerbic of Johnsonian definitions: "In England, [*pension*] is generally understood to mean pay given to a state hireling for treason to his country." Under the circumstances, how could Johnson accept a pension offered by a Whig prime minister on behalf of a Whiggish king? According to James Boswell, Johnson fretted that his enemies would accuse him (as indeed they did) of taking a political bribe. In the end, he did accept: He was grateful for the honor—and the money. But Johnson was always sensitive to the insinuation that the Whigs had purchased, if not his cooperation, at least his silence.

As the eighteenth century moved toward its close, a set of forces came into play that would gradually transmute pensions into something very different from "pay given to a state hireling."

Underlying everything was the philosophical revolution that led up to and accompanied the political revolutions of the 1780s and, in their wake, the Industrial Revolution. In the humanitarianism of Locke and Rousseau, with its stress on individual man, we quickly recognize our own philosophical roots. Less familiar is our enormous debt to the social theorists of the era. To Hume, Paley, Bentham, and the Mills (the "Utilitarians"), and to their friendly opponents on issues of religion, we owe the second root-formulation of American doctrine—that the best society is the one that, under the rule of law, provides the greatest good for the greatest number.

Close ties and common concerns linked the eighteenth-century intellectuals with the scientist-mathematicians of the seventeenth century. The discoveries of such men as Pascal, Graunt, and Halley keenly interested the later thinkers. (Hume, we remember, struggled to encompass and at the same time to circumvent probability theory.) Their concern with the nature of society led them to study "social arithmetic" and to express their key ideas in statistical terms. The very notion of "the greatest good for the greatest number," borrowed by Bentham from Hume, is a statistical as well as philosophical notion. Then too, eighteenth-century English philosophers shared with their predecessors a highly pragmatic turn of mind, an urgent desire to see their ideas applied directly to the social and political ills of the day.

Governments might conveniently ignore the statistical findings of the learned, but businessmen could not and did not. To promote the virtues of protection against "dying too soon or living too long," life insurance and annuity companies sprang up in England and on the Continent. Most were either wagering schemes or outright swindles and soon collapsed. But a few endured. For instance, the Society for Equitable Assurance on Lives and Survivorships, founded in 1762, based its business from the start on actuarially sound principles, survived, and still thrives to this day.

One reason for the success of "The Old Equitable" was the sagacity of its first chief executive, the Reverend Doctor Richard Price. Now nearly forgotten, Price was a genuine celebrity. His sermons—Price was a non-Conformist minister—gained him the patronage of the powerful Whig statesman, Lord Shelburne. His essays on morals earned him the admiration and respect of David Hume and Joseph Priestley. His mathematical writings were read on both sides of the Atlantic. (James Boswell recorded that on September 20, 1769, at a gathering of a club called the Honest Whigs, he met "Price the writer on morals" and Price's dear friend, a visitor from the American colonies named Benjamin Franklin.)

In 1771, Price published a penetrating work in statistical mathematics: *Some Observations on Reversionary Payments.* This pamphlet did for the British government what Jan De Witt's study had done, exactly one hundred years earlier, for the Dutch: It proved that the Crown was seriously undercharging buyers for the annuities it was selling to raise funds. The same year, Price brought out an even more provocative pamphlet, on England's national debt. Both tracts strongly influenced the Whigs in favor of modernizing government finance. But this was only the beginning. In 1773, a member of Parliament named Dowdeswell introduced a bill "for the better support of Poor Persons . . . to grant Annuities for life." The bill was Price's brainchild. Throughout England and Wales, vicars and churchwardens were to solicit funds from their parishioners, invest the money in 3 percent "Consols" (the bonds covering the "consolidated debt" of the Crown), and use the principal and the interest to buy annuities for the needy of the parish. "Any deficiency in the payment of the annuities [is] to be made good out of the Poor Rate": out of local property-tax receipts.

Price's astonishing scheme actually passed in the House of Commons, only to be voted down by the House of Lords. Fourteen years later, in 1787, an expanded version of the idea, calling for the establishment of one central fund supported by both gifts and mandatory contributions, met a similar fate. Nevertheless, Richard Price can fairly be styled the inventor of state-sponsored old-age insurance.

Price knew that the nature of government was changing. As England's overseas trading ventures grew into an empire, government based on the instincts of kings and landed magnates had to give way to government based on fiscal soundness and managerial expertise. Likewise, the institutions of the older agrarian England—the poorhouses and parish taxes—could not be expected to solve the social problems of industrial England.

Between 1743 and 1815, moreover, Great Britain was continually at war, and war, however dreadful, is a great modernizer of government. After a generation of colonial wars in India and the New World, the British found themselves forced to mobilize against Napoleon. To build an army and navy capable of winning at Aboukir (1798), Trafalgar (1805), Corunna (1809), and ultimately at Waterloo (1815), the government had to sweep aside centuries of outmoded administration. Above all, some method was needed to induce senior officers to stand down in favor of younger, more vigorous men. One obvious inducement was a reformed retirement system (the Royal Navy had had a rudimentary system since 1690), including pensions based on rank and length of service.

By 1834, the British state-run pension plans included officials of the Post Office and the Civil Service as well as military and naval officers. Forty-two years after Richard Price's death, his rational approach to what he termed "survivorship" began to win government acceptance. We had entered—but only barely entered—the world of today.

George Washington never received a pension. He was reputed to be rich, and he *was* rich: At his death (1799), he owned forty thousand acres of land in Virginia alone. But throughout his career, Washington worried unceasingly about his financial future. In 1783, asking his cousin Lund Washington for the Mount Vernon accounts, he wrote: "It is not to be supposed, that . . . my public duties, great and laborious as they have been, could render me totally insensible to the *only means* by which myself and family, and the character I am to maintain in life hereafter, is to be supported." And a few months after quitting the presidency in 1797 he was saying rather bitterly to Samuel Washington, who wanted a loan: "I perceive . . . that you are under the same mistake that many others are—in supposing that I have money always at command." He went on:

> The case is so much the reverse of it, that I found it expedient, before I retired from public life, to sell all my Lands (near 5000 acres) in Pennsylvania . . . and . . . in the Great Dismal Swamp . . . to defray the expenses of my station.

Well able to provide for himself, Washington knew that others were less able. He fought long and hard to persuade Congress and the states to honor their financial obligations to the army. He wrote eloquently to the governors on behalf of "that meritorious class of veteran[s]" wounded in the Revolution and awarded disability pensions. "Nothing but a punctual payment of their annual allowance," Washington insisted, "can rescue them from the most complicated misery."[1]

Washington's concern extended as far as his slaves. In his will, he instructed his executors to set up a "regular and permanent fund" for the support of the aged and infirm among them (while they were still enslaved and after their emancipation). And to "my mulatto man, William," the general left "an annuity of thirty dollars during his natural life . . . as a testimony of my sense of his attachment to me and for his faithful services during the Revolutionary War."

George Washington was far from being the only federal official to retire unpensioned. During the whole of the nineteenth century and well into the twentieth, the federal government sponsored pensions for only two classes of recipients: disabled and indigent war veterans (and their dependents) and retired federal judges. For obvious reasons, the veterans had to be accommodated. As for the judiciary, it is a tribute to the astuteness of the founding fathers that they assured in advance the livelihood of the one group of federal officers most vulnerable to bribery.

In *The American Political Tradition,* Richard Hofstadter paints an engaging portrait of this country as it was in the decades before the Civil War.

> Although industrialism had begun to take root, this was still a nation of farms and small towns, which in 1830 found only one of every fifteen citizens living in cities of over 8,000. . . . Factories had been growing in some areas, but industry was not yet concentrated in the factory system; much production was carried out in little units in which the employer was like a master craftsman supervising his apprentices.[2]

Hofstadter can quote a contemporary observer (1836) to the effect that "business is the very soul of an American." But his account reminds us that in the early days of the Republic, business had yet to become the blighting presence it was to become. Thus, Waltham, Lowell, and the other mill towns of New England were the closest thing to the "factory system" developed to date in this country. But if we can believe the testimony of such reliable witnesses as Harriet Martineau (1835) and Charles Dickens (1842), the young ladies of the mills were well off in their jobs. The educational historian Lawrence A. Cremin draws on the recollections of Lucy Larcom (*A New England Girlhood*) for his portrait of life and learning in the mill boardinghouses.

> Most of the boarders came from New Hampshire and Vermont and "there was a fresh, breezy sociability about them." . . . In ad-

dition to receiving informal education from pedlars and phrenologists, the young women attended lyceum lectures, where they heard such speakers as Edward Everett, Ralph Waldo Emerson and John Quincy Adams; they took part in dozens of discussion and study groups; and they studied everything from German to Chaucer to botany in night classes taught by "literary ladies."[3]

As late as 1856, John Amory Lowell could still say proudly of the factory girl that she was no mere slave sentenced for life to her machine. Rather, she had come to work for a few years to earn herself a dowry or to put a brother through college. The money in hand, she would return to the farming or fishing village of her birth and to the young man who awaited her there.[4]

Clearly, such a picture is an idealized one. But even so, in a society still only barely industrialized, on the eve of the Civil War, no strong need was felt for pensions to ease the miseries of old age. People did of course grow too old to work. But in the small communities and the big families of the day, the status of the old was assured. Even the most cantankerous granny had her place by the fire.

All of this was to change. The agents of change were first the railroads and then the war.

In his illuminating book *The Visible Hand,* Alfred D. Chandler, Jr., argues persuasively that "the rail and telegraph companies," not the mills or the mines, "were the first modern business enterprises to appear in the United States." Beginning with the first railroad boom of the 1850s, he traces the emergence and influence of those new organizations. He shows, for example, how railroad financing with its unprecedented demand for capital created Wall Street. "One day in March 1830," Chandler notes, "only thirty-seven shares were traded on the New York Stock Exchange. By the mid-1850s . . . hundreds of thousands of shares changed hands weekly."[5] Most of those were railroad shares.

In similar style, railroad building revolutionized the construction industry. Trained engineers replaced local masons and carpenters. Small builders gave way to great contracting firms like those of Horatio Seymour and Henry Farnum.

Most important, their sheer diversity made railroads utterly new and different.

No other business enterprise, or for that matter few other nonbusiness institutions, had ever required the coordination and control of so many different types of units carrying out so great a variety of tasks that demanded such close scheduling.[6]

To start up a railroad, its managers had to be expert financiers and promoters. To get it built, they had to be skilled designers and engineers. To get it equipped, they had to know mining and milling and the lumber business and how to make or buy every kind of item from steel rails to the mahogany paneling for their "palace cars." While they were learning these things, they had to begin learning the techniques of scheduling, routing, and timing that are basic to mass transportation. Finally, once these matters were mastered, the railroaders could begin the actual business of running the railroad.

By necessity, the railroads created a brand-new type of businessman. "The men who managed [railroads]," Chandler writes, "became the first . . . modern business administrators." They were not entrepreneurs but "salaried employees with little or no financial interest in the companies they served." They saw themselves in a special light.

Because they worked for a salary and not a share of the profits, because they had professional training and had developed professional expertise, their way of life was much closer to that of the modern manager than to that of the merchants and manufacturers who owned and operated businesses before the coming of the railroads.[7]

The Civil War, with its nightmarish problems and its brilliant opportunities, was soon to be upon these early technocrats. But within a decade after the war ended, these men would apply their ideals of mechanical perfection and efficiency to their workers as well as to their machines.

As it gathered momentum, the war thrust industrialization upon both parts of the divided country. The North, more highly industrialized to begin with than the Confederacy, used its industrial muscle as well as its superior numbers to hammer out a victory. Here, one point in particular calls for consideration. The Civil War, fought with modern, mechanized weaponry (including

Samuel Colt's famous revolver, the breech-loading rifle, and the predecessor of the machine gun), was the bloodiest war in history. Indeed, the war was a kind of huge factory for killing and maiming, one that dealt out crippling injuries to tens of thousands of those lucky enough to survive. As the soldiers of both sides lay down their arms and marched—or limped—homeward, the whole nation learned a bleak lesson in what machines could do to men.

Soldiers with wounds received pensions. The fact was not lost on a society already aware that industrialization, like war, exacts casualties. Railroading itself was certainly known to be a hazardous business. As early as 1841, an accident on the Western Railroad, which connected Worcester and Albany, killed a passenger and a conductor and injured seventeen others. The resulting investigation led the line's alarmed owners to reorganize and tighten its entire supervisory structure. Other lines rapidly followed suit. If Alfred Chandler is correct, "the need to assure safety of passengers and employees on the new, high-speed mode of transportation"[8] was the primary reason for the development of managerial efficiency.

The overriding need for safety made the railroads the very first employers to set up pension programs. Nobody wanted to ship his goods—much less travel—on an accident-prone railroad. In hunting for the causes of accidents, railroad executives were forced to take notice not only of badly ballasted roadbeds and overheated journal boxes but also of human failure. As Murray Webb Latimer was later to observe, the possible consequences of employee inadequacy were frightening. They made increasingly clear "[the] advisability of removing from the service elderly persons and others no longer able to perform their tasks efficiently."[9] No less than a malfunctioning switch, a malfunctioning employee had to be replaced.

As a matter of record, the very first formal pension plan in America was put into effect on October 1, 1874, by the Grand Trunk Railway of Canada. But this was a limited effort, covering only the "clerical or indoor staff," about 5 percent of the total work force. A year later, the American Express Company—not a railroad, of course, but a company then closely linked to railroading—initiated the plan now generally accepted as the forerunner of today's pension programs. The American Express plan was "applicable to all who have been in the continuous and exclusive service of this . . . Company for twenty (20) years or more and who have become worn-out or disabled while in its employ." The "worn-out or disabled" received pensions of up to one-half of the average yearly salaries they had earned during the ten years before "discontinuance from service." The company carried the full cost of the plan. Naturally enough, it reserved the right to retire any employee when he reached age sixty "and the sole right to allow or discontinue payment of pensions."

By current standards, the American Express plan can hardly be called liberal. But its very existence was remarkable in the 1870s, and it became an object lesson to be assimilated warily. In 1880, the Baltimore & Ohio Railroad Company became the second U. S. employer to establish a formal pension plan. The B&O did so primarily "to relieve the company . . . from being called upon to make contributions" for the aid of disabled or aged employees. Its plan required employees to contribute. The benefits to the retired (who had to be sixty-five or older) consisted of "an annual allowance for life of ten cents on each dollar [they] paid in," plus an additional half-cent per dollar for each year contributions had been made. For obvious reasons, this formula for recovering their own savings aroused little enthusiasm among employees. In 1882, the secretary of the plan was regretting that "the annuity feature had not prospered in the same ratio as that providing relief for disablements." B&O workers, he scolded, "have not yet realized the importance and value of this form of protection against want in old age."

Indeed, during its first three decades, the pension movement gathered speed about as rapidly as an overladen freight train on a stiff uphill grade. One industrial company, Alfred Dolge, a felt manufacturer, set up a pension plan in 1882; sixteen years later, high carrying costs forced termination of the plan. In 1888, John Wanamaker & Sons, the Philadelphia retailer, developed a plan to cover disability only. As for the railroads, in 1889 there were no fewer than 1,718 of them in the United States, employing nearly 700,000 people; only 6 had pension plans.

During the 1890s, a few more organizations initiated pension plans. The Solvay Process Company was one of them, Consolidated Gas of New York (a predecessor of Con Ed) another. And some of the great American universities began formal pension programs for their faculties: Columbia, in 1892, was the first. Yale, which started its plan in 1897, edged out Harvard by two years.

During the early 1900s, as if in response to an oncoming new era, pension activity increased markedly. In 1900, the Pennsylvania Railroad set up a plan for all divisions east of Pittsburgh. Under this plan, retirement at seventy was to be mandatory for all employees. Those who had completed thirty or more years of service would receive pensions based on the average annual salary of their final ten years. In 1901, Andrew Carnegie, a powerful spokesman in favor of pensions, installed a plan in his Carnegie Steel Company. The next year, Ida Tarbell published her celebrated *History of the Standard Oil Company.* Possibly in indirect response, John D. Rockefeller in 1903 authorized a plan awarding pensions, at the discretion of management, to loyal Standard Oil employees.

From this point on, the list of companies sponsoring pension plans begins to read like a "Who's Who" of American industry. On the roster before World War I were such bellwether concerns as Du Pont (1904), American Stove Works (1910), American Brake Shoe (1911), Beech-Nut Packing Company (1912), American Sugar Refining Company (1912), Atlas Powder (1913), Nicholson File (1914), Winchester Repeating Arms (1915), and the Crane Company (1916). The Associated Press started a plan in 1918; in 1921, the New York Times Publishing Company followed suit. Among other companies instituting plans during the 1920s were American Can (1924), Libby, McNeil (1927), and Gulf Oil (1927). By 1928, according to the National Industrial Conference Board, 244 companies and nonprofit organizations, from Acme Steel of Chicago to the Zion Cooperative Mercantile Institute of Salt Lake City, had set up pension plans.

Thousands of other firms, to be sure, had not. In 1928, we look in vain for a General Motors or a Ford Motor pension plan. No IBM or NCR, no International Harvester or American Cyanamid, no Anaconda or Allegheny Corporation—to mention only a very few—had as yet started a plan. Nevertheless, such was the prestige of those firms that did offer pensions, and of the great entrepreneurs who sang their praises, that the pension concept had begun to be respectable.

These first-generation pension plans tended to have certain features in common. Most of them emphasized disability rather than old-age benefits. The majority were employer financed, and the decision to grant the individual a pension (or to cancel one) most often rested entirely with management.

Once it evolved, the philosophy underlying pensions changed very little over the first fifty years. In 1906, a gentleman named F. A. Vanderlip explained before a charitable conference in Philadelphia why "so many corporations are beginning to provide for their employees in old age."

> The pension attaches the employees to the service and thus decreases the liability to strike. It makes more certain a continuance of efficient men in the lines of work with which they are perfectly familiar. Of quite as much importance is the fact that a pension system enables employers to dispense with the elderly and inefficient and thus gives constant encouragement to good effort on the part of the younger men hoping for promotion.[10]

Mr. Vanderlip went on to cite "the incentive to good conduct" a promised pension presents. He took pains to point out that a pension protects the employer against the possibility of losing seasoned employees to higher-paying competitors. Best of all, these advantages were cheap.

> One great manufacturer states that . . . in his business 1 per cent of the wages fund is sufficient to provide for the necessary pensions, and . . . any business which cannot stand such an increase in expenses is so unstable as to be a menace, rather than a benefit, not only to its proprietor, but also to society.[11]

Andrew Carnegie saw in pension plans a new, sound way to attract good candidates into one of the poorest-paid fields, teaching. Carnegie, by adapting mass-production technology and ruthless marketing to steelmaking, had accumulated one of the world's largest fortunes. He had a great passion for education and poured millions of his dollars into programs for the betterment of teaching. For Carnegie, teaching, like the ministry, was a sacred calling. The good teacher, Carnegie believed, would never crave more than a bare living; in recompense, he should be granted a measure of security in old age. "The least rewarded of all the professions," Carnegie declared in 1910, "is that of teacher in our higher education establishments."[12] Through the Fund for the Advancement of Education, he initiated the financing, for college teachers, of pension benefits that were "portable," or transferable, as the individual moved from institution to institution.

Toward the midpoint of this first fifty years of pension history, a voice even more resonant than Andrew Carnegie's was raised in ardent support of pension planning.

Most biographers of John D. Rockefeller, Jr., agree that a turning point in his life, and in the Rockefeller family destinies, was the "Ludlow Massacre" of April 1914. This was a bloody clash between National Guardsmen and striking miners—many of them employees of the Rockefeller-owned Colorado Fuel & Iron Company—over working conditions and the right to unionize. The guardsmen, shooting wildly, killed forty miners and wounded scores more; the fighting also took the lives of two women and eleven children. Put through a grueling interrogation on his role in CF&I, Rockefeller was able to make good his claim that he bore no direct responsibility for the bloodshed. But the episode convinced him that harsh confrontation between labor and management posed a terrible threat to this country—and to the Rockefeller interests.

Rockefeller demonstrated his courage, and won superb publicity, by visiting Ludlow the year after the killings; the trip included journeys down mineshafts, meetings with the miners, and even a dance. But another Rockefeller response to Ludlow, although it took seven years to materialize, was of much more lasting significance: the formation, in January 1922, of Curtis, Fosdick, and Belknap. Through this private consulting group, Rockefeller became involved in the new field of industrial relations. In 1926, Curtis, Fosdick, and Belknap became Industrial Relations Counselors, Inc. The new firm had Rockefeller aide Raymond D. Fosdick as its chairman and young John D. Rockefeller III on its board.

Like most other industrialists, the early Rockefellers believed that the devil himself had invented the labor union to destroy the old harmony between labor and management and to return society to primal chaos. But Ludlow had taught John D. Rockefeller,

Jr., that violence was the worst possible antiunion strategy. In the long run, enlightened paternalism—in the form of somewhat improved wages and working conditions and of mechanisms for registering grievances—would prove a better weapon. In *The Rockefellers,* Peter Collier and David Horowitz give the gist of Rockefeller-style labor policy. "[A] satisfied labor force meant more profits . . . and any increased costs from accommodating the human weakness of laborers would be more than counterbalanced by increased efficiency and contentment."[13] This was the doctrine Industrial Relations Counselors, Inc., was formed to preach.

In 1929, the firm commissioned economist-actuary Murray Webb Latimer to conduct an elaborate study of pensions in America. The result, published in three volumes in 1932–33, was and still is the authoritative source of information on pension planning before 1930. But Latimer produced more than a compendium. In his introduction, Latimer cited much the same reasons for installing pensions as those given by F. A. Vanderlip a quarter of a century earlier. We've already noted Latimer's insistence on the need to sever the elderly and the inefficient from work forces. But he also mentions that the pension plan is "one means not only of preventing strikes but also of promoting long, loyal and uninterrupted service." And Latimer adds that the "reputation" of a company and its need to "induce capable persons to enter its employ"[14] make pensions especially valuable. A pension plan, in other words, is good public relations. It's a persuasive method of telling the world that you run your business in a civilized, humane fashion.

Despite the Rockefeller endorsement and the prestige of so many of the companies involved, something was lacking in these early plans: money. Very few of those who set up pensions knew or cared anything about pension finance. To the senior executives of the bellwether American corporations, the actuarial discoveries of three centuries were inconsequential. Lightheartedly, these optimists of the Roaring Twenties believed that they could simply go on forever paying the cost of retirement benefits out of current income. Besides, the benefits themselves could be cut off in a moment at the discretion of management. As long as no legal obligation existed, where was the problem?

There were those who disagreed. In a 1925 report, the conservative National Industrial Conference Board was sternly critical of corporate pension policy.

> The great majority of pension plans in American industry have been established with no adequate calculation of their future costs and with no adequate provision for financing them. Humane motives, rivalry, or the expediency of the moment have largely actuated employers in inaugurating their various retirement schemes. But generous impulses ... furnish no guarantee of soundness. And promises that cannot be kept, were better not made at all.[15]

The board's advice was to place pension financing on an actuarially sound basis. In general, the advice went unheeded. Of 307 corporations studied in 1928, only 108 had set aside any financial reserves at all to cover pension obligations. Of these, only 41 had established trust funds to separate pension reserves from corporate capital, the method that is virtually mandatory today. Even where separate trust funds existed, these were invested largely in the stock of the sponsoring corporation.

Latimer himself felt that the unsound financing of most plans seriously undercut their usefulness and credibility. But the onset of the Depression made his admonitions to employers seem silly. By the end of 1931, industrial production had dropped to half of what it had been in 1929. A total of 10 million people, one-fifth of the work force, were unemployed. U. S. Steel had just cut its wage rates by 10 percent for those employees lucky enough to be on call for an occasional day or week of work. Bethlehem Steel had fired 6,000 of the 7,500 workers at its Lackawanna, New York, plant, then "tried to evict them from company housing so that it could be torn down to save property taxes."* Cotton pickers in Alabama and Mississippi were being paid 60¢ for a fourteen-hour day in the broiling fields. Under the circumstances, the fate of a few optional pension plans hardly mattered. Between 1930 and 1935, in fact, the number of employees covered by noninsured pensions actually dropped, from 2.7 million to 2.5 million. Almost inevitably, the Depression focused the attention of the

---

* These examples and many others can be found in *The Invisible Scar* (New York: Pocket Books, 1967), Caroline Bird's searing 1966 study of the Great Depression.

American public not on what private industry had done about retirement but rather on what government might do.

As we've noted, proposals for government-sponsored old-age insurance date back to the eighteenth century, and by 1840, England, France, and other European countries had set up pension plans for military personnel and civil servants. But the first plan for the benefit of a population at large was initiated in 1884 by Prince Otto von Bismarck of Prussia. In 1881, Bismarck had already begun to test in public the idea, heretical for a Junker, that ordinary people needed and deserved financial security in old age. "Why should not the labour soldier receive a pension," he asked rhetorically, "just as much as the man who has been disabled or has grown old in the army or the civil service?" In private, Bismarck was a good deal more cold blooded about his idea.

> One who can look forward to an old-age pension is far more contented and much easier to manage. Contrast a man in private service with one who serves at the chancellery, or at court; the two latter must be far more accommodating and obedient than the former, for they have their pensions to think of.[16]

Whether the Iron Chancellor had in mind "practical Christianity" or (more likely) "ward[ing] off a revolution," not even his biographers are certain. But the fact remains that Bismarck, the absolutist aristocrat, sired Europe's first old age and disability act, which set the retirement age at seventy and provided factory workers and other commoners pensions for life.*

Cautiously, in response to pressure from their electorates, the other major industrial nations followed suit. First came England (1908), followed by France (1910), Sweden (1913), Italy (1919), the Soviet Union (1922), Canada (1927), and Brazil (1934). Then, in the midst of the Depression, the United States launched its own social insurance program, the Social Security System. As we'll see in detail in chapter 6, its provisions, although the product of many compromises between conservative congressmen and President

---

* In *The Arms of Krupp* (New York: Little, Brown, 1968, pages 152–53), William Manchester expresses his belief that the *"Generalregulativ"* of the great weapons maker, which set up a pension plan for Krupp workers, strongly influenced Bismarck's thinking.

Roosevelt's social-welfare specialists, alarmed whole sectors of the business community. Life insurance officials, savings bankers, and others competing for the dollars of those who still had jobs and dollars to save denounced Social Security as a menace to the nation's habits of thrift. Employers were uneasy about the financial stability of the program and unhappy about the payroll taxes they had to pay. Federal and state bureaucrats squabbled over control of the money and over job patronage. Roosevelt himself waxed hot and cold about some provisions of the law. Even the *New York Times* turned against Social Security, editorializing (January 20, 1935) that those in charge of drafting the new law had produced a "debacle." Nevertheless, by early August 1935, the Social Security Act was law.

World War II, which almost overnight snapped the American economy out of its ten-year-long slump, also proved stimulating to private pensions. The main reason was the 1942 executive order freezing salaries and wages "for the duration." Barred from offering higher pay to attract scarce civilian manpower, employers were quick to note that nothing in the order kept them from devising "fringe benefit packages," including pensions. Then too, the combination of high wartime taxes and the tax deductibility of pension contributions meant that much of the cost of a corporate pension plan could be shifted to Uncle Sam. The numbers tell the story. In 1940, the assets of private pension plans totaled about $1.68 billion. Five years later, the assets were worth $3.42 billion. By the end of 1950, their value had risen to $12.1 billion. Over the same ten-year period, the number of employees covered by the plans had risen from 4.26 million to 10.3 million.

At the tail end of this initial spurt of growth came the 1949–50 court case of *Inland Steel* v. *NLRB*. The United States Supreme Court declared that pensions were subject to collective bargaining. This in turn opened the way for the miners, the steelworkers, and other unionized workers to seek pension benefits for themselves. Pensions could no longer be seen as a kind of gratuity to be given or withheld at the pleasure of the employer.

The *Inland Steel* decision ushered in twenty-five years of ripening, a kind of golden age of growth, for private pension plans. Growth, indeed, was inevitable. Between 1950 and 1975, the American labor force grew enormously, from 51 million people to

85 million. Throughout the period, the bulk of the work force, roughly 80 percent, was made up of exactly those working Americans who had the most to gain from *Inland Steel*. Once retirement benefits became bargainable, the employer could hardly deny to his salaried, white-collar employees what he had to provide for his hourly paid, unionized employees. And so, millions of members of both blocs were swept up into the new and existing plans of large corporations. We've noted that in 1950, the number of employees covered by pension plans was 10.3 million. By 1975, the number had risen threefold, to 30 million.

This was the period when today's big pension consulting firms rose to prominence. To cite just one example: During the early 1950s, a gifted executive named Mortimer Dencker alternately coaxed and prodded his conservative partners at Johnson & Higgins, the nation's oldest insurance broker, to get the firm more aggressively into pension work. Under Dencker, J&H was already selling group life insurance and hospital insurance to a blue-chip business clientele. Pension advice was a natural addition to the line, and Dencker made it pay. Pensions were "intricate and expensive," he advised prospective customers. "[Y]ou need qualified pension 'engineers' to help you in . . . design, installation, and operation."[17] Dencker retired, a rich man, in 1966. By the mid-1970s, the J&H pension "engineers" he had assembled numbered about 600 and were contributing an estimated $15 million a year to the firm's earnings.

By the end of 1975, the assets of the country's private pension plans had risen from the $12.1 billion of 1950 to an astonishing $217 billion. This is a fair amount of investment capital. On it is centered the great untold story of postwar capitalism, a story that underlies many of the great *told* tales of Wall Street—that is, the struggle (at first between life insurance companies and bank trust departments; then between the banks and the investment management firms; and finally, among the banks, the investment houses, and the reinvigorated life insurance companies) over who gets to look after this money.

One of the most delicious success stories of the entire quarter of a century is that of the rise to glory of Donaldson, Lufkin, & Jenrette.

Who does not rejoice to hear how three gifted young men

borrowed half a million dollars from their business-school class-mates, founded a new kind of securities firm—one based not on social connections but on *brains*—and worked up the original cap-ital over fifteen years into a 1975 net worth of $50 million? Who isn't beguiled by the bravura of entrepreneurs who dared to list among their corporate objectives, right in the annual report, "To Have Fun"? The reality behind the sparkle was the firm's ability to attract pension- and profit-sharing-fund dollars for it to manage. Part of this ability was indeed sparkle: Invitation-only seminars on pension planning and asset management, luncheons at the Uni-versity Club, addresses by leading economists, and even the firm's unorthodox but spectacular office decor were exercises in impress-ing corporate financial executives and turning them into custom-ers. But hard work played a larger part. As the tools by which securities were sold, voluminous, minutely detailed reports were the DLJ substitute for the gladhanding and backslapping of the traditional customers' man. Finally, there was the willingness of DLJ's young principals to reinvest their profits not in yachts but in the firm itself. For a while in 1969–70, board chairman Dan W. Lufkin, in one of the decade's classic examples of conspicuous consumption, was commuting daily by private helicopter between his farm in Connecticut and his office in New York. But at the same time, he and his partners were acquiring Moody's Investors Services from Dun & Bradstreet to strengthen DLJ's expertise in bond investments.

The results of such dedication were remarkable. In 1962, three years after its start, DLJ was managing about 10 million dollars' worth of pension-fund assets. By 1969, the firm had in hand more than $600 million in pension money. By 1975, Alliance Capital Management Corporation, the DLJ unit formed five years earlier to handle institutional investment, had $1.6 billion under its con-trol. Its clients included such premier corporations as Boeing, Deere & Company, Ford, General Mills, ITT, 3M, Scott Paper, and TRW. In addition, the Moody's division of Alliance was managing pension money for nine of the fifty states. *Inland Steel* and an almost mystically lucky sense of timing had made the three ebullient young men multimillionaires.

In yet another area, *Inland Steel* meant growth—namely, the area of legal regulation. The chronicle of this growth is cloaked in the jargon of accountancy and law and buried in the looseleaf pages of business service reports. In the nature of things, the chronicle is obscure. But in its fashion, the story of pension regulation is no less amazing than that of pension-fund investment. Ever since the end of World War I, the regulation of pension plans had been in the hands of a few brilliant lawyers and accountants in the U.S. Treasury. Their authority stemmed from the Tax Code and from a mimeograph machine. Their sole legal sanction over the thousands of plans in being was their power to cancel the tax-exempt status of any company's pension. And because a cancellation would instantly result in the loss of the benefits for workers, and thus produce a legal and political fireball, the regulators dreaded even the thought of invoking their sole remedy.

Nevertheless, the system worked. To be sure, some rogue corporations have misused their pension funds, risked the futures of their employees, and laughed at the Treasury. Some rogue unions have turned their funds into lending agencies for organized crime. And in the end, regulation by mimeo has had to give way to regulation at once more formal and more punitive. But the fact remains that under the loosest of restraints, employers and unions and their advisors have kept faith with their employees.

Consulting, investment, and regulation are the final links in the long chain that began in Athens, or perhaps earlier, and has wound down through Western social, political, and economic history. Now, instead of dealing with princes and their mistresses, with statesmen and their systems of bribery, we're dealing with an industry. But today's pension industry has an interest of its own. Its workings are fascinating—and its impact on our lives well worth understanding. To probe the workings and measure the impact is the purpose of the chapters ahead.

★ 3 ★

The Pension Industry (I): The Actuaries Are Afoot in the Snow

Kenneth K. Keene has a low-key sense of humor and a nice taste in blue pinstripes. If your image of an actuary involves sleeve garters and a green eyeshade, Ken's style will undoubtedly bend your preconceptions. He *is* an actuary—in fact, a Fellow of the Society of Actuaries. For years, he was head of the pension actuarial section at Metropolitan Life, a job you can't handle if your mathematical training stopped short after freshman calculus. But in Ken Keene's office, there are none of the appurtenances of the professional arithmetician—no bound sets of the society's *Transactions,* no thick looseleaf books full of tables. Above all, there's no desktop mini-computer by Wang or DEC or Basic Four. All actuaries have these, and some even have the Big Apple, the mini that lets you display your data in *three* throbbing colors on the cathode readout. But not Ken Keene. In his office, there's a huge desk and chair and—more important than any computer—one of those executive conversation centers: that is, a couch with a coffee table nearby and a couple of upholstered armchairs—the couch and chairs done up in a mellow chintz, just as in a good club or the living room at home. The conversation center tells you the story. Ken Keene, FSA, is well up there. He is a senior officer, a vice-president and director, of Johnson & Higgins, and one of the two men in charge of the firm's employee-benefit planning department.

If any professional group in America has done well financially, better even than the doctors and lawyers whose incomes dazzle us all, it's the actuaries. The reasons are not far to seek. In the first place, the supply of natural talent is highly limited. The number of mathematically gifted youngsters who can be seduced away from "pure" mathematics and the sciences into the applied math of the actuary is never large. (Recruiting is aggressive. At Michigan, North Carolina, NYU, and other universities with strong mathematics programs, scholarships, well-paid summer work, and handsome job opportunities await those students willing to slog through the arid courses in statistics and probability that actuaries must take.) In the second place, the actuaries themselves, through their closed-rank professional associations, keep a tight clamp on their own numbers. The stringency of their qualification requirements is notorious among the professions. To become a Fellow of the Society, the candidate must study for and pass a set of ten brain-cracking exams covering all of the branches of mathematics. An Associate has to get through five of the ten, and even this can take years. In an average year, only a few hundred entrants gain Associate status, and fewer still become full Fellows. In 1979, there were 104,000 CPAs in the American Institute of Certified Public Accountants. In the same year, 205,000 lawyers belonged to the American Bar Association, and the American Medical Association had 210,000 members. In contrast, the total membership of the Society of Actuaries was just 7,000, and this is double the 1970 figure. Of the present members, about two-thirds work for insurance companies. Only about 2,200 can be classified as consulting actuaries specializing in pension work.

Coupled with the enormous growth in pension planning, this scarcity explains why actuarial trainees with only two or three exams under their belts can haul in $20,000 salaries and command some remarkable fringe benefits. Among these are sabbaticals, graduate scholarships sponsored by the Society, and long, *long* paid vacations to be spent in attendance at mathematics seminars.

And Big Apple computers on which to have fun with all the pension arithmetic.

And this in turn begins to explain Ken Keene.

In the pension-consulting trade, the actuary always used to be, by tradition, Mister Inside. That is, he was the technician, the boffin—withdrawn, scholarly, quite possibly moody or "different"—who dwelled in the back room where the calculators and the clerks were, did his dance with the numbers, and rarely, if ever, ventured forth into the daylight. The Mister Outside who handled the all-important client contact and the marketing of the firm's services was very often not an actuary at all. He'd be styled an "account executive" or "consultant." But in fact he was a salesman pure and simple, somebody hired to bring in new business for the actuaries to work on and to guard the firm's established accounts against the predations of competitors. To a Fellow of the Society, the outside men might be quite nice chaps, and important ones, too. But they were, after all, tradespeople. Always, their promises to clients would bear watching.

Tucked away in their back rooms, actuaries had plenty to do. As we noted in chapter 1, setting up a new pension plan calls for the close study of the group to be covered and a steady eye for the design of the basics of the plan: eligibility, the benefit formula, and so on. But this is only part of the job. In addition, the actuary must put in place the financial underpinnings of the plan. So important is this side of actuarial work that it justifies a digression, one long enough to open up the intriguing subject of pension finance.

How much will a pension plan cost? Like the exact whereabouts of an electron in physics, the cost of a pension plan is one of those bemusing facts that can only be known in retrospect. The ultimate cost, plainly, will be whatever amount of money it takes to pay every last dollar's worth of pension benefits to every last qualified employee and employee beneficiary. Indeed, as long as the plan's sponsor is a going concern, hiring new employees to replace those who retire and in due course bringing the new employees into the plan, the day will *never* dawn when the final entry is made in the great pension ledger and the true cost of the plan stands revealed.

This is the sort of response that gives treasurers heartburn.

Treasurers don't want to know about atomic physics. What they *do* want to know is how much money to set aside each year to meet pension obligations as these fall due. Also, for the sake of their own budget planning and forecasting, they want their actuaries to project these obligations over the short term: over the three years or the five years that lie just ahead.

Actuaries certainly can come up with these more empirical figures. (In the flat phrase of Shepherd A. Sheinkman, a senior actuary of the Martin A. Segal Company, "They're the guts of the practice.") But to do so, an actuary must first do certain other things. He must make estimates, the so-called actuarial assumptions, about the key events likely to overtake the plan. He must decide on a *funding method* for the plan and decide, too, on the length of time over which, by means of this funding method, the plan's *unfunded liabilities* are to be paid off. These terms sound technical and *are* technical, and some pension specialists like to surround them with a degree of mumbo jumbo. But none of them is hard to understand.

"Lots of things can affect a pension plan," says Barnet N. Berin, the actuarial director for William M. Mercer. "But only a few really matter."

What matters the most, Berin adds, is the rate at which the plan's assets will earn interest. Everything else being equal, the higher the interest rate, the lower will be the contributions needed to meet plan costs. Often—although not always—this state of affairs is extremely pleasing to the actuary's client. In pension affairs as in love affairs, moreover, little things mean a lot. If the actuary tells his client that next year the pension assets will probably earn 9 percent instead of 7 percent, the 2 percent rate increase will *de facto* produce a 28 percent increase in actual yield. This is no small difference.

Other factors also matter. For instance, salary levels (and thus pension benefits) rise with inflation. The actuary who wants to help his client peer accurately into the future must therefore make an assumption about the rate of the rise and its effect on plan costs. And he must make similar guesses (actuarial assumptions, although highly educated and based on statistical analysis, are nevertheless still guesses) about the effects of such other plan "events" as employee turnover, preretirement mortality, and the likelihood of change in the age at which most employees will elect to retire.

In quieter times, a set of actuarial assumptions, once made, tended to stay unchanged for years or even decades. The assumptions were the guidelines by which those in charge of the pension plan managed the plan, and the guidelines were blessedly, reassuringly stable. If the actuary set 5 percent as the interest rate the assets could reasonably earn, the investment people down at the bank were delighted to shoot for 5 percent. A 4 percent return would have been worrisome, of course, but so would one of 6 percent. And 7 percent would have been unhealthily speculative: "much too warm" for a pension fund.

Of course, if any of the actuary's assumptions had proved *wrong* (if, for example, only half as many employees had left their jobs as the actuary had assumed would leave), it could have been changed. But *wrong* was not a term nonactuaries customarily leveled at actuaries. If the actuary himself detected a significant discrepancy between his own assumption and the unfolding experience of the plan, he might make an "adjustment," or a series of adjustments, in the assumption. But he might also persuade his client to change the plan.

Alas, the days have fled when actuarial assumptions could be chiseled like sacred writ into the cornerstones of client offices and trust companies. In these degenerate times, the interest rate on one of the world's safest investments, the six-month bills issued by the U.S. Treasury, can get up to the mid-teens. Now, pension costs are taking big, big bites out of corporate incomes and shareholder profits, and this makes treasurers look very hard indeed at what the actuaries are saying and wonder if perhaps the actuaries shouldn't be saying something different.

To capture the changed situation in all its delicacy, one member of the profession, now retired, has coined a charming simile. "It's like a small boy," he says, "dragging a sled over a field of new snow. The boy's footprints will wander, but their path will be obvious once he's finished his walk. But the sled tracks will curve along, sometimes on one side of the footprints, sometimes on the other. Actuarial assumptions are like the sled tracks, rarely right on target but always being corrected by the pull of experience." Few other actuaries have this man's gift for imagery. But his little prose poem does leave one question unanswered: Who (or what) does guide those wandering footprints? We'll come back shortly to this question and the troubling lack of an answer.

Given the current actuarial assumptions, enough time, and a sharp pencil, a pension actuary can work up, for anybody in a pension plan, the benefit payable at retirement and the lump sum needed to cover the cost of all the benefit payments. What's the best way for the employer to accumulate the money? In theory, the employer, if he were rich enough, could do it all at once. That is, he could plunk down *today* a sum large enough that with interest added in, over the years it would come to equal the lump sum needed at retirement. At the opposite extreme, the employer could run a plan with no advance funding at all. As each employee retired, the employer could simply begin to pay the monthly benefits out of current income. As long as the income held up and the rate at which people retired stayed steady, there would be no problem.

But few employers can afford to set aside all the pension money at once. Few employees would settle for pensions contingent on the continuing profitability of their ex-employers. For both sets of parties to pension plans, it makes sense to spread the costs over as many years as possible. So the actuary must devise for his client a funding method that lets the client spread the costs, and keep on spreading them, in an orderly, advantageous way.

Because the choice of funding method helps determine the employer's tax-deductible pension contributions year by year, the IRS sets limits on the types of methods allowed. And because the security of the benefits depends on the slowness or speed with which the cash to back them up is set aside—and this is what funding methods are really all about—ERISA, too, regulates funding methods and their use. Here, there's no need to go into the fine differences among the various funding methods. It's enough to understand that these differences are basically differences in one area, the treatment of a pension plan's *past-service liabilities.*

In the footnote to page 20, we noted the importance of the *past-service* concept, which to pension planners means the amount of time employees have worked for their employer before the pension plan came into being. Most pension formulas take past service into account. (Not to do so would almost certainly mean discriminating against older employees, most of whose service has already been given by the time the plan starts.) A moment's thought will show you why past service is so important in pension financing. Suppose the company you've worked for for the past ten years puts in a new pension plan. Carrying the cost of your benefits for your future service is easily done on a current basis. Year by year, as you "earn" the benefits, the company puts aside the money to pay for them. But the instant the plan is started, the benefits for your *ten years of past service* also become plan obligations. True, they won't be payable until you retire, but the company must still find the money for them somehow. Until it does, your benefits aren't *fully funded* and thus completely secured. Multiply your own example by those of all the others in the plan and you can see why dealing with this overhanging past-service liability takes tender, loving actuarial care.

The actuary's funding method must provide a way to pay off the past-service liability a little at a time while keeping the company current on future-service benefit contributions. The rate of liquidation can't be too fast (the IRS would object)* or too slow (the yearly payments might not cover the cost of benefits falling due). Past-service-liability totals can be huge sums of money. According to a November 1977 *Fortune* survey, 10 of the top 100 American companies "have unfunded . . . liabilities equal to a third or more of their net worth." Among these companies was the faltering Chrysler Corporation, with a net worth of $965 million and unfunded pension liabilities (almost all for past service) of $1.1 billion. International Harvester's net worth was $772 million, its unfunded pension liability $676 million. Lockheed Aviation had a net worth of $189 million, unfunded pension liabilities of $276 million. Does this mean that these companies, and others in similar circumstances (including, perhaps, your own), are in a state of financial emergency, or will be unable to meet their pension bills? Of course not, insist the actuaries. Says Bob Berin: "If the actuary is making conservative assumptions, monitoring actu-

---

* In the view of the IRS and Congress, allowing too rapid a rate would permit companies to avoid taxes by pouring money into their pensions during periods of extremely high profits.

al experience, and making changes, and if the pension cost—which includes amortizing past-service liabilities over twenty to thirty years—is acceptable [to the client], then there's nothing to worry about." Even *Fortune,* which views the situation with alarm, points out that "the bulk of the unfunded liabilities are concentrated among a relative handful of companies" and adds, "actually, the employees have little to fear." As *Fortune* sees it, the ones with problems are the shareholders. With pension contributions rising at the rate of 15 percent a year and eating into profits, their dividends suffer. And under ERISA, if a company doesn't find its pension cost "acceptable" and is forced to terminate a plan, the government has the right to go after shareholders' equity to help pay off the liabilities. But this is a story for another chapter.

Cooking up pension formulas, setting up actuarial assumptions and funding methods, and then, each year, reporting in great detail to clients on what their plans have cost and will cost truly is, in the Sheinkman phrase quoted earlier, "the guts" of the actuary's job. There are also other assignments. For instance, actuaries sit on both sides of the table in labor negotiations, to supply their clients with cost data on any pension changes that come up for consideration. Increasingly important is the role actuaries play in mergers and acquisitions, where the values of the pension assets and liabilities that will change hands directly affect the nature of the deal. In sum, there has been no shortage of work in those actuarial back parlors.

As the 1960s wore on, successful actuarial firms began to swim in work (and money) and found themselves in need of "boss actuaries," men able not only to make the numbers dance but also to manage people. A "boss actuary" has to be something of an impresario. In a field where talent is in chronically short supply, he has to be able to find new talent—and, at need, to lure established practitioners away from the insurance companies, the government, and the competition. For this, the essentials are good academic contacts, a wide acquaintanceship within the profession, and a flair for making one's own firm seem superior to all others. Then, too, the "boss actuary" must be a successful boss. He has to match the right subordinates to the right accounts, pacify the prima donnas on his staff, hire support personnel, open branch offices, and all the rest. Few people clever at mathematics are also naturally clever at management. But a handful have proved to be very good indeed.

As consulting firms began to shape up their management structures, two other things started to happen. One of them was the computer. In the computer's infancy, the senior actuaries in most firms not unnaturally regarded the computer sourly, like cavalry generals contemplating their first tanks. The things could be useful, one could certainly see that. But the cost, man, the cost! And besides, were those clumsy machines really proper tools for gentlemen?

As recently as the mid-1960s, most pension records were still being scrivened up by hand in corporate insurance or personnel departments. The major computer operation in pension work was the job of converting such "manual" data into meat for the computer, a boring task that required no mathematical skill whatsoever. In those days, the actuaries would look on benignly while the computer people scurried around with their trays full of punch cards. The more highly strung actuaries would worry. What if a bus smacked into the truck carrying the cards to the processing center? Great Pythagoras! Thousands upon thousands of irreplaceable employee records, spilling out of their cartons onto the sidewalk, becoming folded, becoming *mutilated,* lost forever! Undoubtedly, a problem. Yet, not a problem that mattered *professionally,* that changed the arithmetic.

It was the younger actuaries, the enrollees and the associates, who were curious about the computer. They were the ones who took the night courses, who studied machine language and programming and began to work on projects that *did* change the arithmetic—or rather, that speeded up the arithmetic so much that the nature of actuarial work itself had to change as a result. For instance, consider the labors of Russell L. Millman. Millman, a Johnson & Higgins pension actuary, toiled for *four years* over a program that would let him and his colleagues computerize the actuarial valuation reports they provided their clients each year. When you remember that every pension plan has its own formula, its own set of actuarial assumptions, and its own past history, you realize why Russ Millman lost weight and why his jaws ached from clenching his teeth. Along with the inevitable errors that creep into any long, complicated computer program, Millman had to put up with the skepticism of his superiors and the tolerant amusement of most of his associates. "It was awful all the way," he recalls, "but I did it." And it worked.

By this time, it was the 1970s and punch cards were no more. Instead, there was magnetic tape and disk storage and *floppy* disk storage. The major actuarial consultants all had their own computer centers smelling of machine oil and their own special actuarial software. Assignments that used to take a roomful of clerks and trainees a week or more (for example, adding up all the benefits paid out during the year past) could now be done in hours. The old generals had retired, and the new generals dreamed about tanks every night.

The second of the events that changed the makeup of consulting firms was a sudden shift in the way the people who bought corporate services wanted to do business. This *bouleversement* can be very simply defined as "Let's get rid of the middleman." It started in the late 1960s and spread rapidly through the service trades. For example, take advertising. For decades, advertisers had happily relied on account executives to be liaisons between themselves and the oddball types who actually dream up and produce ads. Then, one fine day, everything was different. Nobody wanted to talk to account executives any more. Instead, the client wanted to rap directly with the copywriter. Or with the art director who told the girl how to paste up the layouts. Never mind that the writer was a *descamisado,* a hairy shirtless one who lived on Dexedrine, or that the art director, being by definition a visual creature, had absolutely nothing coherent to say. The idea was to get ever closer to the creative people. They were the ones who cut the cane, and everybody else was a mere *gringo.*

Human nature and the profit motive being what they are, there very soon emerged on Madison Avenue a new subspecies of copywriter, hirsute and picturesque as ever but spellbinding on the aims and goals of advertising. Just as soon, art directors began to speak with the tongues of angels on the new modalities of visual communication and the need to build them into the budget. Like old women in Russia looking for twigs in winter, out-of-work account executives shuffled around in search of writing assignments—want ads, menus, *anything*—so they could qualify for "Copy/Contact" jobs and get back into the game.

On Wall Street, the flight from the middleman was complicated by the back-office crisis of 1968, when the sheer volume of trading threatened to drown the brokers, and the ensuing epidemic of insolvencies, mergers, and reorganizations. It still is complicated, as the securities industry struggles to get all the way back into the modern world. One result has been the proliferation of the so-called discount brokers. These firms, with such names as Quick & Reilly and Source Securities, go after the "heavy hitters," the seasoned private investors who play the market like a Wurlitzer. "A really heavy hitter," says Jeffrey W. Casdin, the founder of Source Securities, "can easily throw off five grand a year in [brokerage] commissions." To build up a clientele of such sluggers, Casdin and his competitors offer only one thing: the execution of orders to buy and sell, at rates as much as 80 percent cheaper than those charged by, say, Merrill Lynch. "How do we do it?" asks Casdin rhetorically. "Easy. We don't give away fancy research and we've fired the customers' men."

Pension consulting is a less volatile business—to put it mildly—than either advertising or stockbroking. Even so, the pressure to deal directly with the specialists has grown steadily stronger. One reason is cost. According to a survey in *Business Insurance* (December 12, 1977), pension consulting firms were charging their clients fees that ranged "from $30 an hour up to a high of $400 an hour. . . . Most of the hourly rates cited were between $50 and $125 an hour." Today, of course, the actuaries are asking more still. With the meter ticking away at rates like these, the clients want to be sure that every minute is productive. Another reason is that pension clients today are better educated than they once were, more familiar with actuarial concepts (and the trends in accounting and law that affect them), and no longer in need of hand holding by an intermediary.

The computer, then, has freed the actuary from the mechanical aspect of his work with numbers. (Less than a decade ago, actuarial firms really did have back rooms where figure clerks ground out pension computations on small, desktop calculators.) The growth of the market for actuarial services has taught the actuary how to be a manager as well as a mathematician. Client pressure has done the rest. Ken Keene of Johnson & Higgins chats easily about the changed role of the actuary. Norman R. Minor, an Associate of the Society and a J&H senior actuary, chimes in: "We're primarily designers of benefits. There certainly have been changes, and the pension situation is very fluid. One thing it's produced is a lot of inequity at the higher end of the pay scale." And Minor explains cheerfully the "Executive Equality Plan" the people at Johnson & Higgins have designed and are presenting to clients as a remedy.

That the $150,000-a-year executive is faring more poorly under the pension-plan system than is the $15,000-a-year blue-collar worker is an intriguing notion—especially to $150,000-a-year executives. Furthermore, the notion may even contain a measure of truth. But when Keene and Minor write in *Executive* magazine (Fall, 1979) that "*a special layer of benefits is necessary simply to remove that discrimination* [their italics]," one's eyebrows do twitch upward. "Designers of benefits"? Perhaps so, but these designing gentlemen are a long way from Pascal and de Moivre and Richard Price. Indeed, they've left the actuarial realm far behind and have entered the even wealthier kingdom of marketing.

Similarly, at the New York headquarters of William M. Mercer, Bob Berin's executive conversation center is upholstered in magnificent off-white sueded leather. Berin, too, must deal with clients. His elegant office is an impressive backdrop for his gently voiced but effective efforts at persuasion.

There is, of course, nothing too alarming about the fact that in a few pension consulting firms Mister Inside has become Mister Outside, or that actuaries as a group are growing more involved in the sales end of the business. Times *have* changed, and circumstances with them. It's appropriate for the actuary to emerge from behind the scenes and, in Bob Berin's nicely turned phrase, "demythologize his own role" in the pension-planning system.

Yet, there's no doubt that this new visibility is bringing with it some problems, not the least of them the erosion of the actuary's longstanding and indispensable independence.

Within the profession, it's an open secret that some clients expect their actuarial firms to make the right kinds of adjustments in their assumptions at just the right time. This expectation is not new. In one celebrated instance back in 1971, U. S. Steel so arranged matters with its actuary* that its pension contributions dropped by $42.7 million (about 41 percent). Adding this amount

---

* The actuary simply increased the interest assumption by 20 percent, raising it from 5 percent to 6 percent.

to pretax earnings meant that U.S. Steel could report an $8-million increase in earnings rather than a $35.7-million decline for the year. Such episodes were common enough to force a bitter comment from the lips of one actuary. In 1972, James Curtis, president of the very large actuarial firm of Milliman & Robertson, told the trade journal *Pensions* (spring, 1972): "Some companies treat an actuary as though he were a legalized bookie. They just want us to get figures together that will help their profit picture."

ERISA has supposedly reformed all of this, by requiring actuaries to "certify" pension assumptions and funding methods and to explain changes in them. But the effectiveness of the law is dubious. In 1976, two years after ERISA became law, Caterpillar Tractor's negotiations with the United Auto Workers gave rise to a pension increase. But Caterpillar's actuaries changed both the interest assumption and the wage assumption on the UAW plan. As a result, Caterpillar's pension expense for the year could be lowered by $6.6 million, or about 5 percent. And its unfunded liability was reduced from $440 million to $270 million. Were these changes, so comforting to the shareholders, justified by the actual experience of the plan? Who can tell? Neither Caterpillar nor its actuaries would disclose the new assumption figures.

At this writing, an even more astonishing assertion of client supremacy is the subject of gossip in the pension trade. It seems that Hoffmann-La Roche, the huge and secretive Swiss-owned pharmaceuticals company, has turned over to its own computer experts the job of adding up all of the pension figures needed for its U.S. tax and other filings. Hoffmann has, in effect, prepared its own actuarial valuation report. The company, according to Ken Keene of Johnson & Higgins, is now making the rounds of this country's consulting actuaries, to try to find one that will supply the needed certifications. Says Keene: "I guess the actuary will be allowed to test Hoffmann's figures, like an auditor. But I don't know. We wouldn't want to do it, for sure." Will Hoffmann find an actuary flexible enough to do its bidding? "I wouldn't bet against it," Keene says with a smile. And his answer stands. Nobody in his right mind *would* bet against an actuary.

There are many other ways in which an agreeable actuary can assist a client in his business dealings—at the expense, when all is said, of the pension plan and those dependent upon it. One of the most intriguing examples of such actuarial helpfulness involved the Bendix Corporation of Detroit and a much smaller company, Tulsa-based Facet Enterprises, Inc., which Bendix first created and then spun off to its shareholders in April 1976, at the behest of the Federal Trade Commission.

To satisfy the FTC, Facet, originally a group of Bendix divisions, had to be a "viable, competitive company"; and so it was, on paper. Bendix started off the new company with a seasoned management and assets worth more than $40 million. But Bendix kept quiet about some things that didn't show up on the balance sheet and thus never aroused the interest of the FTC. In particular, Bendix said nothing about pension assets and liabilities. The Wyatt Company, Bendix's actuarial firm, allocated to Facet $14.8 million in pension assets, which it claimed was enough of a start on the funding of Facet's 41.6 million dollars' worth of pension liabilities. As a conscientious professional, J. Perham Stanley, the Wyatt actuary in charge, would have told his long-time client, Bendix, of some big problems lying ahead for Facet. But neither Stanley nor Bendix ever told the Facet people that they could expect a rash of early retirements, coming on the heels of the benefit enrichments Bendix had privily negotiated with the UAW, to upset the balance in the pension fund between contribution income and benefit outflow. Only when Facet became independent and hired its own actuary did it learn the truth: Instead of putting $2 million a year into its pension plans, Facet would have to contribute at least $4.5 million a year for the next five years, and maybe longer. The difference was the difference between a "viable, competitive company" and a chronic loser.

Seething, Facet chief executive James B. Treacy fought doggedly to keep his company afloat while seeking a legal remedy. For reasons it has never disclosed, the FTC refused to open the Facet case. Luckily for Facet, the IRS, after listening to the actuaries for both sides, reacted differently. In October 1979, the IRS approved a settlement under which Bendix agreed to turn over to Facet another $17.5 million in pension assets, enough to lower Facet's yearly contribution burden by $1.7 million.

J. Perham Stanley acknowledges that the ratio of Facet's pension assets to its liabilities was low. In a November 1978 interview, he told me that if he'd been representing Facet, he might well have protested exactly as Facet's actuaries had done. But before Facet became independent—that is, before April Fools' Day, 1976—there *was* only one client, Bendix, and only one pension plan, the Bendix plan. As Bendix's actuary, therefore, he was bound to remain silent. From an independent professional with professional standards to maintain, this is the thinnest of answers. From a fiduciary whose primary obligation (according to ERISA) is to the employees in the plan, Stanley's answer seems to me something worse than thin.*

How much juggling with assumptions and fiddling with funding requirements actually goes on? Very little, say the indignant actuaries, and it's hard to argue with them. Even under ERISA, it can be impossible to determine whether an increase in, say, the interest assumption is genuinely warranted by the past investment performance of a plan or is merely being adopted to ease the pressure on an employer's earnings. Some actuaries have indeed blamed ERISA itself for creating new opportunities for slippery behavior. Consider: ERISA specifies that only federally "enrolled actuaries" can certify the required triennial plan valuation reports. To become an enrolled actuary, an individual must pass two examinations. These are administered by a board under the control of a group called the American Society of Pension Actuaries. The Society of Actuaries was much annoyed by these provisions of ERISA. To the Fellows of the Society, who have sweated out their seven or nine or ten exams (the number has grown over the years), ASPA was an upstart organization and the government's program a slap in the face. An enrolled actuary could be a nobody, a mere figure clerk. What such a person might do to land and keep a pension account was anybody's guess. Only in 1979, after five years of grumbling, internal debate, and bickering with ASPA, did the Society of Actuaries consent to join the board supervising the enrollment program.

To be sure, the temptations and pressures confronting actuaries today also confront the members of the other professions. This is an era, let us bear in mind, in which surgeons pocket something like $300 million a year for snatching out the tonsils and adenoids

---

* These paragraphs make use of the detailed account of the Bendix-Facet pension imbroglio I wrote for *Fortune* (January 15, 1979).

of over 600,000 children, an operation medical authorities deem almost never necessary. We live in a time when lawyers run ads offering cut-rate wills, cheapie divorces, and pistol permits. Ours is the age when George J. G. Goodman, the "Adam Smith" of *The Money Game* and *Supermoney* can quote the (unnamed) "head of one of our major drug companies" as declaring with smiling cynicism that "one good accountant is worth a thousand salesmen."

When all professions are putting themselves up for sale, why pick on the actuaries?

Part of the reason, surely, has to do with the problem of accountability. Venal doctors, engineers, accountants, and their kin in the other professions leave traces of their venality and irresponsibility in the community. They can be caught. Although it's not easy, they can be subjected to professional discipline and to action by the courts. But the pension actuary is different. He need never even try to cover up the traces of his malfeasance: The technicalities in which he trades are beyond the reach of all but a very few. If the actuary does wrong, years and decades may elapse before the consequences come to light. Who, then, can bring him to book?

The heart of the reason is even more important. On the actuary's nicely tailored shoulders rests the ultimate responsibility for the soundness of private pensions. Other professionals—the employer's lawyers and accountants and investment advisors—may want the pension plan to be operated as part of, or at least in the closest concert with, the employer's business interests. But a pension plan is not a profit center. The actuary's unique role is to say no to its treatment as such and to anything else that might jeopardize the safety of the benefits. In a business society that wants everybody to say yes to the boss early and often, saying no is a tough job. But somebody's got to do it.

The combination of great responsibility and the lack of any ready remedy for misfeasance is a heavy burden for any professional. We may well be demanding too much of the pension actuary. Being human, and therefore fallible and prey to temptation, the actuary does not always measure up. A few years ago, the noted business writer John Brooks summed up actuarial vulnerability with great tact and charm.

Too often, the actuaries have seemed to be filling the role of validator of bad or questionable practice—a role rather like that of a medieval king's priest, whose job it often was to confer the mantle of holiness on temporal power, to tell the king and the world that what the king did was right.[1]

And so, we come back to the question raised by the parable of the boy and the sled. If actuarial assumptions, like the sled, "are rarely right on target but [are] always being corrected by the pull of experience," what higher reality governs experience? As we've seen, the most important element of this reality is investment results: what happens to the money already in the pension fund. It's time we took a look at what *does* happen to those pension dollars.

★ 4 ★

The Pension Industry (II):
The Money Managers

We can start with an ad in *Dun's Review* (November 1979), a magazine for financial executives. In Eugene Saxton's witty illustration, a man wearing a blindfold is perched on the edge of his office desk. In the man's right hand is a dart, which he's about to throw in the general direction of a dartboard on the wall. Standing in the doorway are two executives. One of them is saying to the other, ". . . and Smedley here is our pension fund manager." Whether Smedley's dart lands in the section of the board labeled "Index Fund," the one labeled "Real Estate," or any of the others is, we're meant to see, entirely a matter of happenstance.

The idea is that "you can't just farm out your corporate pension funds and rest assured." Above all, you can't rely on those hit-and-miss trust companies and asset-management firms. You need Metropolitan Life to guarantee you a good return, "over 9 percent," on your pension fund. The Metropolitan gets you this from its "mixture of sound, dependable assets," five-sixths of it bonds and mortgages, which is worth *in toto* a comforting $40 billion.

Without debating the merits of the Metropolitan's claim,* we can recognize the ad for what it is: another volley in the unending tripartite skirmish for a bigger share of the country's pension investments.

In the beginning, there were only two parties to this warfare—life insurance companies and bank trust departments—and they started off about even. In 1950, according to *Pension Facts* (an annual handbook compiled by the American Council on Life Insurance), life insurance companies controlled 5.6 billion dollars' worth of pension assets, while banks controlled $6.5 billion. By 1960, the insurance companies had fallen well behind, and asset-management companies were starting to nibble away at bank pension business. That year, insurance companies held $18.6 billion in pension assets; banks and other asset managers, $33.1 billion. In 1970, the score stood: insurance companies, $41.2 billion; their competitors, $97 billion. And in 1978, the most recent year for which figures are available, the insurance companies are still lagging far behind. They control pension assets worth $119 billion, but their competitors control $202 billion.

During the early years of pension growth after World War II, employers could see strong reasons to put their pension funds in the hands of the insurers. Such companies as the Metropolitan, the Prudential, and the Equitable Life might be hyperconservative investors, earning 4 percent or less a year on their portfolios, but they were safe and unassailably strong. Besides, life insurance companies had the actuaries and the key-punch systems to help them keep tabs on a plan and the administrative machinery to process the retirement claims as they flowed in.

But insurance company pension plans were inflexible, and their ironclad guarantees made them expensive. Even more important, insurance companies were prohibited by law from investing more than a tiny fraction of their assets in common stocks. The banks were quick to take advantage of these handicaps. Their trust-department representatives pointed out suavely that because pension funds were trust funds, they as professional trustees were the

---

* Although in October and November 1979, the U.S. government would pay any amateur with $25,000 or more to invest the equivalent of 10.9 percent or better on its ten-year agency bonds.

logical people to handle the money. The life insurance companies fought back hard. They won federal tax exemption for their pension-asset earnings in 1959, and in the early 1960s they gained the right to set up so-called separate accounts for pension assets and to invest these freely in common stocks. But this was of little avail. As matters sorted themselves out, the insurance companies held on to the pension-investment accounts of some of the wealthiest and largest American corporations (Bell Labs, International Harvester, Standard Oil of Indiana, Campbell Soup, TWA, for example) and of some of the smallest (life insurance agents sold individual-policy pension plans to tens of thousands of little businesses). But everything in between—and much of the big stuff besides—went to the trust companies.

Schadenfreud means "joy in another's sorrow." As the pension business really began to grow in the 1960s, insurance company investment specialists undoubtedly felt a heartwarming surge of *Schadenfreud* watching a new, upstart breed of asset manager begin to do to the banks—albeit on a smaller scale—what the banks had done to the life insurance companies. From Jean Lambert and Fred Mates to Peter Vermilye and Gerald Tsai, the charged-up young men who went scrambling after pension accounts even used the same arguments. Trust departments? Well, yes, they *were* competent at the routine work of investment.* But they were too rigid, there was too much division of authority and too much red tape. Above all, the banks weren't making their pension clients very much money.

Good salesmen that they were, the asset-management people knew better than to mount frontal attacks against longstanding bank alliances. Instead, they'd tell their prospects: Look here, we wouldn't *dream* of asking you for all of your business. But we do have an approach to equities (or bonds or whatever) that's just a little bit different. We've done rather nicely with it, too. Why not let us show you, at almost no risk? Give us just 10 percent of your fund to work with . . .

---

* There's an enormous amount of this routine. For example, according to Martin Mayer (*The Bankers*), in the early 1970s, Citibank's trust department was processing 600,000 stock-market transactions a year and clipping "literally millions of [bond] coupons."[1]

Employers listened, and they thought: If we're going to split up the fund, why split it up just two ways? Why not three? Five? Why not give each of a group of investment advisors a handful of dollars and see who comes out ahead? For that matter, why not hire our own "in-house" investment experts, assign them a chunk of the pension fund, and see how well they do?

Today, very few major employers use only one investment advisor on their pension funds. Most *Fortune* 1000 companies, certainly, use more than one. Some use five or six. Indeed, in 1979 the Ford Motor Company was parceling out its $5.1-billion pension fund among no fewer than eighteen advisors. This group included ten banks, seven asset-management firms, and one life insurance company (the John Hancock), all of them brand-name institutions. Even companies with only 100 to 500 employees sometimes use more than one pension-investment counselor.

The result of this fragmentation of the market has been a severe challenge to the banks, great prosperity for some asset-management firms and lasting prosperity for a few, and a recent upsurge in insurance company pension-investment activity. Thus, in 1974 the Morgan Guaranty Trust Company of New York looked after $14.5 billion in pension assets, Citibank handled $14.2 billion, and Bankers Trust $11 billion. All told, these three banks managed nearly $40 billion, a little over 17 percent of all of the country's nonfederal pension reserves. But by the end of 1979, Morgan Guaranty was overseeing $14.9 billion, the Bankers Trust share of the action had dropped to $9.6 billion, and that of Citibank was down disastrously, to $7.5 billion. The total, $32 billion, was lower by 20 percent than the total of five years earlier. And it represented less than 10 percent of the $328 billion in U. S. pension funds.

In this huge-scale game of musical money, the life insurance companies, for reasons that will become clear later, have been big gainers. Metropolitan Life, which in 1974 managed 7 billion dollars' worth of pension assets, now (1979) manages $12.5 billion. Equitable Life has increased the pension assets under its management over the same period from $7.5 billion to $18.4 billion (the increase includes the $1.4-billion Central States Pension Fund of the International Brotherhood of Teamsters). The Prudential has done almost as well as the Equitable. Pension assets under its supervision have risen from $9.8 billion in 1974 to $18.4 billion in 1979.

Of the asset-management firms themselves, none at present are in this league. Brown Brothers Harriman & Company manages 4.7 billion dollars' worth of pension assets. T. Rowe Price Associates of Baltimore manages $4.4 billion. Lionel D. Edie & Company of New York (owned by Merrill Lynch) looks after $3.8 billion. And Alliance Capital Management Corporation handles $3.7 billion, much of it in state and municipal, not corporate, funds. But some twenty other firms each control a billion dollars or so, and dozens manage pension portfolios worth $200 million to $500 million.

No one knows how much money the pension moneymakers make, but the aggregate must be huge. When I raised the question over the telephone, Philip Metcalf, Director of Marketing for Lionel D. Edie, flinched almost audibly. "You're going to have a good deal of trouble getting that information," he said tartly. What he meant was, You'll never get it. And he's quite right. The figures aren't available anywhere.

Creatures of regulation that they are, bank trust departments publish the fee schedules on which they base their money-management charges. The rates are there for all to see. But while the individual pension client knows perfectly well what *he's* paying, neither he nor anybody else knows what others are paying, because the amounts under management are not revealed. Only the banks know, and the banks are not telling. If the money manager is a life insurance company, not even the client may know what the charge is for this service. Traditional forms of insurance-company-designed pension plans don't as a rule separate investment fees from other administrative charges. Indeed, puzzling over an insurance company's annual pension statements has driven many a young assistant treasurer into the way of madness. One of the chores a consulting actuarial firm expects to do for clients with money in insurance company hands is prepare reports that explain the reports of the insurance company.

Like banks, asset-management firms issue schedules of their charges. These charges are computed on a sliding scale: That is, for the first ten million dollars under management, the annual fee might be 0.3 percent, or up to $30,000; for the second ten million,

0.25 percent; and so on. Many firms charge extra for such services as economic forecasting and measurement of the fund's investment performance against those of other funds. The fee schedules are hardly deep, dark secrets. "I might let you have one if I liked you," says Lionel Edie's Metcalf cautiously, but in fact a request typed on a corporate letterhead will almost certainly produce a schedule. Actual billings to clients are another matter.

There are a couple of special reasons why the pension fund investment business is particularly profitable. The main one is that by its nature, a pension fund is always growing. As long as its sponsor stays in business and keeps up its plan, there will be more millions to invest. Then, because the gains on pension fund investments are tax free, the growth of a pension fund will be more rapid than that of, say, a trust fund for the benefit of a wealthy family's children.

Of course, dreadful things can happen, as they did in 1974. That was the year that the value of the employee-benefit-fund assets under Morgan Guaranty's management dropped from $14.1 billion to $10.6 billion, a loss of 25 percent. "The dominant factor in the decline," Morgan Guaranty wrote—deadpan—in its annual report, "was the erosion of stock prices. It more than offset the net inflow of funds from investment income, new business, and contributions to employee benefit plans."

In fairness to Morgan Guaranty, the 1973–74 bear market victimized virtually every other institutional investor. To cite just one parallel example: In 1974, Endowment Management and Research Corporation and other asset managers supervised a $56.1-million drop in the endowment portfolio of Yale University. This negative performance was exceeded only by that of 1973, when Yale's endowment had slid downward by $78.1 million. The two-year total loss represented 22.5 percent of the value of the entire endowment. (If you're old fashioned enough to be wondering what supposedly conservative institutions such as pension funds and universities are doing with so much money at risk, wait a while.)

But whatever the state of the economy and the securities markets, the business of investing pension assets continues more or less steadily on its course. It's a rewarding business. "A hundred million dollars isn't a very large fund by our standards," Frank Burr observes, "but it's a *lovely* living." Indeed it is. The fee for managing $100 million might be $400,000 a year. On this amount of income, a couple of hardworking investment people can run as much of an office as they need and still make themselves $100,000 or more a year. No wonder the banks each year lose a trickle of their brightest and best investment managers to the asset-management firms. No wonder these firms in turn are steadily losing their more independent-minded portfolio managers, who go off into business for themselves, taking with them if they can their choicest accounts.

To understand what these experts *do* with all the money, you need to think first about the nature and uses of a pension fund. Not to belabor the obvious, the purpose of a pension fund is to be the source of pensions—that is, of lifetime incomes that will be the chief support of large numbers of elderly people. A fund set up to do this will thus have a sizable number of beneficiaries. Payments to these beneficiaries will flow forth over years and decades. (In contrast, a family trust fund may well have only a few beneficiaries, and payments may come due all at once: for instance, when the beneficiaries come of age.)

What *should* one do with a fund that's supposed to take care of a lot of people over a very long time?

The classic answer begins with the advice given by Benjamin Graham, the first, the most brilliant, and perhaps the wealthiest of all securities analysts. According to the pseudonymous Adam Smith, in *Supermoney,* the Graham counsel is simple: "The first thing you must do is not lose your money."[2] To bring about this happy outcome, so different from what happened in 1973–74, the wise investment manager should take pains to spread his investment risk. First, he should diversify in terms of the *types* of investments in his fund—holding some common stocks, some preferreds, some bonds, possibly some mortgages, and so on. Next, he should diversify over a wide range of industries, so that a bad year in one may be offset by good years in others. Then, he should diversify geographically, lest droughts, earthquakes, or man-made disasters in one narrow region jeopardize his entire portfolio. Lastly, the sage investment manager should stretch out his investments over time. By making sure his holdings mature at intervals, he can avoid being forced to reinvest at times when the economic news is unfavorable.

A portfolio run according to these rather Polonian principles might not contain the hottest stocks on Wall Street. It might not hold the private-placement notes of the most aggressive conglomerates. It might be empty of high-yield real estate paper. But it would be *safe*. And until about 1963, safety—not rapid growth nor yet high "total return"*—was considered the *sine qua non* of pension fund investment.

Don't think, however, that the cautious disciple of Benjamin Graham would steer clear of stocks altogether. In his books, Adam Smith makes much of the celebrated "Bundy Report" of 1967. In this remarkable document, McGeorge Bundy, then president of the Ford Foundation, took colleges and universities to task for their antediluvian investment practices. "We recognize the risks of unconventional investing," Bundy said, "but the true test of performance in the handling of money is the record of achievement, not the opinion of the respectable." If you need money to help offset inflation, don't come to the Ford Foundation. Sell your bonds and put the proceeds in common stocks. From the exhortation, surely one of the silliest pieces of advice ever given to the American academic community, Adam Smith dates the beginnings of institutional fascination with the stock market.

In fact, pension managers had been putting money in the stock market since the early 1950s, and doing so at a rate that some observers found alarming. By 1952, the Senate Committee on Banking and Currency was saying nervously that "pension funds [were] probably ... the largest current purchasers of common stocks." In 1954, pension funds absorbed 27 percent of all the new stock issued. By the end of 1957, the funds held 6.6 billion dollars' worth of stocks, an amount equal to 40 percent of their total assets. In *Pension Funds and Economic Power,* a 1959 study for the Twentieth Century Fund, Rev. Paul P. Harbrecht, S. J., was fretting that "the build-up of property in the pension funds" would lead to something very bad called "the paraproprietal society," in which socioeconomic power would vest entirely in the institutions

---

* "Total return" takes into account not only the dividend of a stock each year but also the increase (or decrease) in the market value of the stock. Whether this makes sense or not, in the absence of the actual sale of the stock, is open to question.

that controlled (without actually owning) all the common stock in the country.

This has yet to happen, perhaps because money managers are less interested in wielding socioeconomic power than in trying to make more money on their portfolios. But what did happen in the 1960s was almost as bad. The money managers in general and pension fund managers in particular forgot all about Benjamin Graham. As fiduciaries, people in charge of other people's money, they were supposed to behave like "prudent men."* But inflation supplied them a ready rationale for behaving instead like fantan players. In inflationary times, said the rationale, the world is perverse. As the declining dollar undercuts the values of the old "safe" bonds and high-dividend stocks, these become in reality the least safe investments of all. *Au contraire,* the safest investments are those with the best chance of going up in value as the dollar goes down: to wit, common stocks—and volatile stocks at that. Therefore, paradoxical as it may seem, during inflationary times the truest fiduciary, the most prudent "prudent man," is the speculator.

And so, instead of diversifying to spread investment risk, the money managers of the 1960s narrowed the range of their investments and embraced risk lovers. Well before "Mac" Bundy, they did sell their bonds and load up on common stocks, to the point that stocks made up 85 or 90 percent of their portfolios. They did more. They took the pension funds into real estate. Not into conventional mortgages, under which you lend a reputable landlord money that he repays year by year, principal and interest, out of the cash flow his property generates. No. Into deals involving direct ownership of office buildings and shopping centers and hotels built by developers with high hopes and low rates of occupancy.

With great verve, Adam Smith and John Brooks and other writers on finance have chronicled for us the mad investment world of the 1960s. They deal lovingly with its fecklessness and its grandiose promise and with the rise to power of the institution-

---

* The term stems from the 1830 court case of *Amory* v. *Harvard,* in which Justice Samuel Putnam held that a fiduciary "is to observe how men of prudence, discretion, and intelligence manage their own affairs" and to do likewise with the funds under his own control.

al investor over the individual, the "little guy" who used to be called "the backbone of the market." They introduce the people—some of them gifted, some of them callow, and not a few of them shameless rascals—who did the actual recommending, buying, and selling. With cautionary gusto, they reminisce about the dogs and cats that the professionals—no less than the amateurs—bought with avidity. What stocks! Parvin Dohrmann, a casino operation that went from a 1969 high of $142 a share to a 1970 low of $12.50. The infamous National Student Marketing: from $91 to bankrupt. Commonwealth United: from $25 to $1. And Levin-Townsend Computers: from $68 to $3. Yet, amid all the color and drama and spectacle, the *results,* what really happened, tend to blur.

Take 1968. This was the year, according to John Brooks (in *The Go-Go Years*),[3] "when speculation spread like a prairie fire." In the first five months of the year, Brooks notes with awe, "Merrill Lynch opened up over 200,000 new accounts.... One American in every thousand—counting men, women, and children—opened a new brokerage account *with a single firm.* " In 1968, some stockbrokers "had personal commission incomes ... running to more than $1 million." As the banks and insurance companies and asset managers moved in and out of the market like pachyderms bumping around a circus ring, block trades of hundreds of thousands of shares became commonplace and forty-million-share days set new trading records.

So, what did happen? Specifically, as the Dow-Jones average climbed to 985 in December, what happened to the 106 billion dollars' worth of pension funds the professionals had under their management? The answer is a colossal anticlimax. In 1968, U.S. private pension funds gained in value at the rate of ... 6.5 percent. That's not much better than the 5 percent you could get yourself at the local savings bank. ("Are you kidding?" said my wife. "With that kind of money, you should get 5 percent plus at least a toaster.") Furthermore, that 6.5 percent is the best the pension funds did during the entire period from 1961 through 1978. The next best result was that of 1977, 6.4 percent, gained at a time when the savings banks were offering 6 percent and *two* toasters. In the terrible year already mentioned, 1974, pension funds actually lost half a billion dollars, which made their rate of gain from investments and new contributions *minus* 0.4 percent. The figures also suggest that the results for the 1960s were a lot better than those for the 1970s. From 1961 to 1970, the yearly increases averaged 5 percent. From 1971 through 1978 (the most recent year for which figures are available), pension assets went up by an average of 3.5 percent a year. Over the whole period, the average result was a not very impressive 4.4 percent.

(Of course, there's always the possibility that the numbers themselves are crazy. The asset figures used to compute these results come from the Securities and Exchange Commission's *Statistical Bulletin*s, and I have it on very good authority that the SEC's research is not what it used to be because the staff has been cut from sixteen to an overworked six and the budget slashed to the bone. The figures for contribution income and benefit outflow are the work of the Social Security Administration. But the nice lady who used to compile these has either retired or quit and isn't compiling them anymore. Nevertheless, all the statistics in question are published—without disclaimer—by the American Council of Life Insurance and are considered both reliable and authoritative by the people in the pension industry.)

To reject Benjamin Graham, to plunge headlong into speculation, and to suffer all the agonies of the gambler for the sake of a 4.4 percent return seems like one of this era's great exercises in futility. A dangerous exercise, too. Don't forget: This money that goes roller-coastering up and down in the stock market is *pension* money, the very same money people are counting on to save them from the poorhouse when they get old. As a matter of fact, one of the oddest things about the past twenty years of pension-investment history is that almost nobody has squawked about the poker being played with the nation's old-age money. Once in a while, it's true, somebody has said something about investment procedures. In 1962, William L. Cary, chairman of the SEC, put forward proposals for tightening legal regulation of the stock market. In 1965, William McChesney Martin, head of the Federal Reserve Board, told a commencement-day audience at Columbia University that he detected "disquieting similarities between our present prosperity and the fabulous twenties" and that this boom might end as disastrously as had that one.

In *Supermoney,* Adam Smith quotes David Babson, an old-line, conservative money manager, on the causes of the 1970 market collapse. Babson had already labeled the stock market "a national crap game" and a "gigantic pari-mutuel operation." Among his villains in 1970 were "corporate treasurers who looked upon their company pension funds as new-found profit centers and pressured their investment advisers into speculating with them."[4] Needless to add, the investment advisors were only too happy to cooperate.

In all of this time, the strongest voice to be raised on the issue of pension investment has been that of an actuary. William M. Mercer, as we've already noted, is one of the best known of the country's actuarial consulting firms. It's also the biggest, with 2,300 employees including 185 actuaries. The Mercer president is a Scot, a well-tailored, tough Glaswegian with a shock of prematurely white hair. He signs his name "A. J. C. Smith," but everybody knows him as "Ian Smith." Writing in the business section of the *New York Times* (Sunday, April 17, 1977), Ian Smith opened up the investment problem with the precision and dispatch of a surgeon. "The results of pension fund investment in North America during the last decade have been disappointing." He listed the various explanations put forward for this poor performance: "a business recession, continuing inflation, the unpredictable behavior of the stock market or, less kindly, incompetent investment management." Then, Smith probed the real problem, which was not so much one of incompetence as of irresponsibility.

> When the wrong people, members of the investment community, are asking the wrong question—"How can we get the largest return on investment on these funds?"—getting the wrong answer is almost inevitable.

"Pension funds," Smith reminded his readers,

> are accumulated savings for pensioners and sometimes for widows and orphans. They should not be treated as counters for scorekeeping in a trading game devised by the investment community.

Smith called for a return to "old-fashioned fundamentals like the determination to preserve capital and the expectation of continuity and growth of income," and he challenged plan sponsors to accept their responsibility for investment policy.

Responsibility cannot be left in the hands of Wall Street. An introspective institution concerned with the technicalities of trading financial instruments is not best suited to taking care of the futures of our citizens, without some direction.[5]

Smith did say that ERISA, with its stress on the fiduciary relationship of the investment manager to the pension fund, was having "a significant and beneficial effect." But the suggestion that only a federal law would serve to discipline investment management was hardly a compliment to the investment community.

When the head of the nation's largest actuarial firm delivers so stinging a commentary on the practices of his brothers-in-arms in pension investment, you expect a lively chorus of response. In fact, there was none. No organization of pensioners or of the about-to-be-retired named Ian Smith its "man of the year." No securities-industry group, *per contra,* bellowed its outrage. No pension sponsor stepped forward either to agree or to disagree. No government body declared its intent to launch an investigation. In sum, the people who in 1974 lost 21 billion dollars' worth of pension assets in the stock market shrugged off the loss and went on playing the same game of musical money, and no one paid any attention.

During the later 1970s and on up to the present, the game has become, if anything, more complicated. Some employers, alarmed by ERISA's fiduciary requirements, have tried to dissociate themselves entirely from the investment process by giving their investment specialists absolute discretionary power over the pension money. Others, convinced—probably rightly—that they would be considered fiduciaries no matter what, have held on to all or some of the decision-making power. Still others have been more concerned about what was happening to the money itself. As we've seen, quite a number of these have turned away from banks and asset-management firms to the supposedly more cautious life insurance companies.

The life companies have elbowed their way back into competition largely through shrewd marketing of so-called "guaranteed investment contracts." Under such a contract, a life insurance company takes over and manages a portion of the customer's pension assets, guaranteeing a stated interest return. At the end of the contract period, which may run for three years or for up to twenty years, the company returns the principal and interest to the pension fund. With guarantees currently at levels of 9 percent and sometimes higher, the arguments in favor of GICs are proving persuasive. (One problem is that the customer can't get his money out, without hefty penalties, until the contract term is up. Another is that the insurance company may be studiedly vague about what *it* makes on the deal. Insurance companies are not eleemosynary organizations.)

But the most striking complication has been the growing prominence of a relatively new, specialized type of go-between, the pension financial consultant. Under the theory that corporate pension administrators know too little about investment and have too little time to seek out expert investment management, the financial consultant, or "pension consultant," screens out and evaluates money managers. In the late 1960s, pension consulting acquired a dubious reputation. Some firms did an honest job, but others earned most of their money not from their corporate clients but from the money managers themselves. These operators simply recommended whichever asset managers they could persuade to kick back to them in return.* As time ran on and ERISA came into being and the recommendations turned sour, some of the sleazier consultants dropped out, leaving the field to such legitimate firms as Frank Russell & Company of Tacoma, Washington (the largest), and Evaluation Associates of Stamford, Connecticut.

Why do some of the nation's biggest companies turn to outsiders for pension-investment evaluations they could probably do all by themselves? For an answer, listen to Stephen Rogers, one of the founders of the six-consultant firm of Rogers, Casey & Barksdale. "There are two reasons. First, we get our clients to *think* about money-market structures. Then, we get them to *think* about capital markets." Steve Rogers feels that about "three-quarters of our clients are okay, investmentwise." But even those clients need advice on "stripping out" inconsequential pension assets from the main bodies of their investment funds (the current RC&B buzz word for this process is "immunization"). Once this is done,

---

* Sometimes the kickbacks took the form of brokerage commissions directed to the broker that owned or was favored by the consultant. Sometimes the kickbacks were plain cash.

RC&B finds money managers for its clients who will approach the equity markets with "purity."

In terms of marketing, the RC&B methodology has been a great success. In 1976, when consultants John Casey and Edgar Barksdale joined Steve Rogers to start the firm, the three men began with six clients of Rogers's former firm, Dreher & Rogers. Using a blend of salesmanship and something they dubbed "the active/passive approach" to portfolio management, RC&B by the end of 1979 had signed up forty-five customers, including such big names as Celanese, CBS, Eastman Kodak, Honeywell, PepsiCo, and Singer.

Success has made RC&B some powerful enemies, among them the influential monthly *Institutional Investor.* In its January 1980 lead story, the magazine's Anise Wallace accused Casey and Barksdale of having threatened to sabotage the computer program of a firm where both formerly worked, in an effort to get more money. (Instead, Wallace said, they got fired.) Wallace also made much of John Casey's rudeness toward portfolio managers and RC&B's supposed devotion to two pension-asset-management firms, Batterymarch Financial Management and Fayez Sarofim & Company, her implication being that these firms were doing something in return for referrals. Also, Wallace claimed that some RC&B clients were being made to pay heavily for a computerized portfolio-analysis system that the firm would be able to sell to other clients.

Steve Rogers flatly denies all of these charges and says he has tapes to prove Wallace knew the truth. He acknowledges that RC&B was "devastated" and John Casey "deeply wounded" by the article. However, "our clients have been wonderful," he says bravely, adding that two of them, Gannett Publications and the Tribune Company, have helped with legal and public relations advice.

Why the attack? *Institutional Investor,* it helps to remember, considers itself the voice of the money-management business, including trust-company and insurance-company investment departments as well as asset-management firms. These are the very organizations that Rogers, Casey & Barksdale makes a living supervising. In my opinion, the magazine's editors have chosen this way of warning RC&B and other consultants—in no uncertain terms—not to push quite so hard.

Unfortunately, the intensity of the attack blurs the real question. For all their suavity (and Steve Rogers has the presence of a master salesman) and their talk about "immunization" and "purity of approach," do the RC&B people and other consultants offer a genuine service or merely some elegant, backfield ball handling? The present writer isn't really sure.

Never mind. We're now in the 1980s. Money managers have invented such supersophisticated investment techniques as M.P.T. (Modern Portfolio Theory) and the even more incomprehensible beta theory, both of which look as if they ought to be taught only in graduate mathematics seminars. Computers now handle not only the mechanics but the timing of buys and sells. And always, the consultants are watching—waiting like wolves to eliminate the weakling managers from the herd. Surely, this should mean that pension funds are at last being invested with brilliance. Are they? Listen to the experts. In early February 1980, Lewis M. Eisenberg, a Goldman, Sachs & Company partner, was telling the *New York Times* why the stock market had suddenly come alive. "What has happened," Eisenberg said, "is a reverse in investing psychology. . . . Psychology plays a tremendous part in the price of stocks. . . . There is also a dominant fear of missing out as the market rises." Psychology? Fear of missing out? So much for the computers.

Later in the very same month, another Goldman, Sachs partner had something to say to the *Times.* Leon G. Cooperman, chairman of the investment committee, declared: "Within a year from the time stocks reach their 1980 peak, cash equivalents, and quite probably bonds, will be outperforming stocks." So much for General Motors, which had just told its pension fund managers to get up to 70 percent of their portfolios into stocks.

Plus ça change . . .

Perhaps the grandest investment absurdity to date is the deal, consummated in August 1979, between huge Citibank and auctioneers Sotheby Parke Bernet. Writing in *The International Art Market* (October 1979), Howard L. Katzander described the arrangement as

a seminal contract under which the auction house will advise the bank of investment opportunities in fine arts and antiques for its

most important private clients—those with $1 million or more to
allocate to the art market.

Just one month earlier, Katzander noted, the Labor Department
had changed its interpretation of the "Prudent Man Rule" to allow pension trustees to invest pension money in fine arts. Donald
L. Rundlett, the Citibank senior vice-president who will admin-
ister the art investment program, told Katzander that "pension
fund investments [were] not covered by the [Sotheby Parke Ber-
net] contract." But Katzander suggests that it's only a matter of
time. In an editorial he pointed out that in Britain, Peter Wilson,
chairman of Sotheby Parke Bernet Ltd., became advisor to the
British Rail Union Pension Fund in its $85 million investment in
art and antiques. Can American pension funds be far behind in
their eagerness to take advantage of the booming market in paintings, sculpture, antiquities, old furniture, and other valuables?

O Mercury! The idea that pension money managers, prudent
men all, will now be adventuring amongst the Ruysdaels and Cri-
vellis and Charles Cressents is enough to freeze the blood.

Abraham Lincoln was absolutely right. You can't leave war to
the generals.

★ 5 ★

Public Employee Pensions: Whose Side Is the Sheriff On?

When David Crumley Bevan, the Haverford- and Harvard-educated chief financial officer of the Penn Central Corporation, decided in the late 1960s that it was time to milk that shaky enterprise for his own benefit, his milking machine was the Penn Central's $300-million Supplemental Pension Plan. Bevan simply had the plan, of which he was chairman, buy at premium prices from a small syndicate—consisting of himself and a few of his colleagues—the shares of such non-blue-chip companies as Kaneb Pipeline, Tropical Gas, and University National Bank of Florida. The shares, needless to say, had cost Bevan and his pals almost nothing. Buying cheap and selling dear to your own pension fund is always a splendid way to turn a profit.

Bevan, it seems, had no monopoly on this special method of making a pension plan yield juicy preretirement benefits. According to a civil suit the Securities and Exchange Commission filed in November 1979, Charles G. Bludhorn, the prince of *conglomerateurs,* had been doing exactly the same thing at his company, Gulf & Western Industries. That is, Bludhorn had been using the pension fund to make "inappropriate" investments in companies in which he personally held sizable interests. For example, the G&W pension fund reportedly acquired 32,000 shares of Bohack Corporation stock at a time when Bludhorn and Don F. Gaston, his executive vice-president, between them owned 8 percent of Bohack. The pension fund later sold the shares at a loss.

(Bludhorn emphatically denied any wrongdoing. He labeled the SEC complaint a "cynical and misleading" interpretation of perfectly straightforward business transactions. And on his behalf and that of Gaston, G&W retained Edward Bennett Williams as its legal representative.)*

Much more notorious has been the systematic despoliation of the Central States Pension Fund of the International Brotherhood of Teamsters. According to Steven Brill,** the fund has paid out over $1 billion of its $1.4 billion in assets in the form of real estate loans—at highly preferential interest rates—to friends and relatives of key Teamster officials and to Mafia-linked gambling interests. In time, this unsavory traffic will probably impair the fund's ability to cover the costs of the pensions payable from it. But even Brill acknowledges that press accounts have overstated the Teamster problem.

> The most basic error involved reports that failed to distinguish between the Central States fund and other Teamster pension funds, thereby implying that all Teamster member pensions were in trouble when, in fact, they weren't.[1]

Brill points out that a number of Teamster pension funds, including that of the Western Conference, which is the largest union fund in the country, are absolutely free of taint.

Clearly, private pension plans, union and nonunion, are vulnerable to the venality or criminality of those in charge. (ERISA has helped, but as we'll discover later, ERISA is weakest in the area of enforcement.) Just as clearly, while many instances of manipulation and embezzlement have come to light, many more remain undiscovered. Nevertheless, few would argue that the private pen-

---

* In October 1980, the case, according to the SEC attorney, Fred Freedman, was still in its early stages and was being "hotly contested."
** Brill's *The Teamsters* contains a mass of information about the Central States fund as well as a closely reasoned explanation of the consequences of its lending practices.

sion system is hopelessly corrupt or so badly run as to cry out for a total reform.

Unfortunately, this argument *can* be made to apply for another major sector of the nation's retirement resources. Indeed, it's almost an understatement to say that the system of pensions covering the country's 12 million federal and 13.5 million state and municipal employees is, in the words of *The Reader's Digest* (March 1976), "a nationwide scandal."

Fueled by ignorance and greed on the part of so-called public servants and by expediency on the part of the congressmen, mayors, and governors who control the money, the benefit levels of federal and other public pension plans have soared out of sight. Today, thousands of retired public employees are bringing in more money, via their pensions and Social Security, than they were earning just before they retired! Some pension provisions, like the length of service required for a full pension and the qualifications for a disability pension, are so loosely written and so gently enforced as to turn thousands of public-employee plans into giveaway programs, a form of welfare for hale-and-hearty ex-cops, firemen, and sanitation hands.

Not even felony convictions keep civil servants from collecting their pensions. Illustrating the point in bold type is the sorry tale reported by at least two Connecticut newspapers and by the *New York Times* (February 29, 1980). It seems that in New Britain, Connecticut, twenty-three city officials, including the police chief, the fire chief, and two former Civil Service commissioners, have been arrested on various charges of bribery, extortion, and perjury in connection with the sale of city jobs. (According to reporter Bill Neagus of *The New Britain Herald,* who has been covering the investigation since its start in 1979, "the forgery charges have been dropped because of the statute of limitations.") So far, eleven of these officials have pleaded guilty. Understandably disturbed by these developments, Mayor William J. McNamara has tried to discipline his straying associates. Among other things, he has sought to block their pension benefits, but to no avail. To quote the *Times:*

> The Hartford law firm of Shipman & Goodwin held that "New Britain may not deny pension benefits to such employees," and

that the city charter and the Connecticut Municipal Employees Retirement Fund excluded denying pensions even to those found guilty of crimes.

Although the costs to the taxpayer of public-employee pension plans are literally immeasurable, it's possible to determine—more or less—where we stand today: In 1978, the contributions to these plans totaled $33.7 billion, and contributions are increasing at the rate of $4 billion to $5 billion a year.

In some areas, the bite is already crippling. In New York City, pension costs soak up more than forty-five cents out of every dollar of property-tax revenue. (We'll see shortly why *Fortune* has conferred upon New York's "pension dilemma . . . the status of a contemporary legend.") Across the country in Los Angeles, over *half* of the city's property taxes go for the pensions of city employees. San Francisco's per-employee pension costs are among the highest in the country. Detroit and Boston spend much of what they bring in on pensions. And the worst is yet to come. According to the facts and figures that federal government specialists and their consultants are only now beginning to assemble, most state and local plans are seriously underfunded. Their contribution levels, high as they are, have failed to keep pace with their skyrocketing benefit levels.

In the saddest shape of all are the plans covering federal employees. Of these, the biggest is the Federal Civil Service Retirement System, which includes nearly five million people, has assets of over $60 billion, and is costing the public nearly $16 billion a year. In 1977, its actuaries reported unfunded liabilities of $107 billion. After adjustments that allow for recent peggings of benefits to the Consumer Price Index, this figure could be as high as $200 billion. "By some estimates," *Fortune* reported in November 1977, "the unfunded liabilities for federal-employee pensions will soon reach the trillion-dollar mark." But nobody, in government or out, really knows for certain the financial status of the federal plans. Not until 1979 did Congress pass a law requiring the yearly actuarial valuation of federal pension programs.

So deep is the twilight surrounding public-employee pension plans that the federal government itself isn't sure how many such plans there are. Until 1975, most pension experts thought there were about 2,300 of these plans. That year, S. Howard Kline and Russell J. Mueller, in charge of the Pension Task Force of the House Committee on Education and Labor, began to gather data for the *Task Force Report on Public Employee Pension Systems*. They sent out thousands of their twenty-two-page questionnaires to local government bodies across the country. To their astonishment, about 6,700 came back, in varying stages of completeness. But not even the authority of Congress was enough to persuade everybody to answer. Said Russ Mueller, not very upset: "I'd guess there are between 500 and 1,000 plans, most of them small ones, that didn't reply."

Among the thousands that did reply are plans of all sizes. They range from the New York State Employees' Retirement System, with over 400,000 participants, to tiny programs like the insured plan, costing about $10,000 a year, for the 11 employees of Salisbury, the small, northwestern Connecticut town where I live.

Only 379 of these plans can be classified as large ones, covering 1,000 or more employees. At the state level, 68 plans had assets of $50 million or more in 1979. (The number of state plans is greater than the number of states because many states have separate plans for their teachers.) Seventy-one county and municipal plans were worth $50 million or more in 1979.

The big-city systems in particular are mazes. If you work for the municipal government of Los Angeles, for example, you might belong to any one of four plans, each with its own rules, benefit levels, and funds. Chicago employees may find themselves in the Cook County Employees' Annuity & Benefit Fund (1979 assets, $236 million), the Illinois Municipal Retirement Fund ($1 billion), the Municipal Employees' Annuity and Benefit Fund of Chicago ($503 million), the Park Employees Annuity & Benefit Fund ($132 million), the Policemen's Annuity and Benefits Fund of the City of Chicago ($426 million), the Public School Teachers' Pension & Retirement Fund of Chicago ($700 million), the Retirement Plan for Chicago Transit Authority Employees ($297 million), or the Sanitary District Employees & Trustees Annuity & Benefit Fund of Chicago ($75 million).

New York City claims to have a mere fifteen separate retirement systems for its 350,000 employees. Eight of these are run according to actuarial rule, while seven are operated on an *ad hoc*

or pay-as-you-go basis.* But as CUNY Professor Damodar Gujarati points out in his 1978 study of New York City pensions,
things are even more complicated than they look. The biggest of
the eight actuarial systems, the New York City Employees' Retirement Plan,

> is actually an amalgam of four subsystems, each of which has its
> own retirement plan and benefit structure. These subsystems cover
> career employees; transit operating employees; uniformed sanita-
> tion employees; and transit police, housing police, and the uni-
> formed correction force.[2]

So, New York is in fact running eighteen different retirement programs. Some of these have picturesque names and intriguing
pasts. The Police Pension Fund, Article 2, for example, is (according to Professor Gujarati) "the oldest public pension system in the
country." It was founded in 1857, and originally the pensions for
"New York City's finest" were financed by the proceeds of city
sales of unclaimed goods. Then, there's the Grady Law Retirement Plan. This one—simply—provides benefits for "officers and
employees of the city" who are not entitled to the benefits of
another city retirement plan. Who Grady was, deponent know-
eth not.

Why the proliferation of plans and programs within one city or
state? Part of the reason lies in a primordial truth (maybe *the* primordial truth) of American government—namely, that no bureau
or department or office of government will ever willingly place itself at the mercy of any other bureau, department, or office. This
extreme devotion to the doctrine of the separation of powers can
be summed up simply in the memorable phrase you can hear on
any day in the locker room of any station house in the land: "Only
cops understand cops." (For "cop," you can of course substitute
"sanitation man" or "building inspector" or "high-school indus-
trial-arts teacher" *ad infinitum.*) In practical terms, this means
that the day will never dawn when a policeman submits his ap-
plication for, say, a disability pension to a board dominated by
transit workers or firemen.

---

* In fairness, the nonactuarial plans cover relatively few city employees and are
maintained chiefly to take care of employees who retired decades ago.

There is, to be sure, another powerful reason. When I asked a veteran of Connecticut small-city politics, "Why all the separate plans?" the man eyed me as if I had taken leave of my senses. Finally, convinced of my earnestness, he said, "More jobs, dummy." Even then, I was slow to react. How could multiplying the number of pension plans multiply the number of local-government jobs? It took me a moment to grasp that the more pension plans there are, the more boards, committees, subcommittees, hearing examiners, and appeals commissioners there have to be. And the more clerks, typists, secretaries, office boys, messengers, and (a sign of the times) computer operators. The people who get these jobs tend to be grateful—shall we say—to the politicians who create the jobs and keep them in the budget.

Finally, we have to keep in mind that public employees, be they policemen, highway department laborers, maintenance men, or whatever, *love* their pensions. The pension is the part of the job that makes up for its monotony, its low pay, its lack of opportunity, and in some cases its physical danger. As a child at the tag end of the Depression, I can remember overhearing family gossip about relatives who had taken city jobs or had gone into teaching "for security." "So-and-so will never make any real money," my father would say, "but he'll never get fired and he'll get his pension." Exactly. And it's not at all surprising that people who care this much about their pensions will want to protect them by locking them away in separate systems run by their own kind.

But to see why these plans are in such serious trouble today, we have to look beyond both patronage and self-protection, into some fundamental facts about the public payroll. The first of these is simply its growth. At the federal level, in 1950 federal employees covered by the Civil Service or other federal retirement plans numbered about 1.7 million. In 1978, the number was 2.8 million. If not the nightmarish mushrooming some politicians like to label it, this increase is still substantial. At the state and local levels, however, the growth in public employment has been astounding. In 1950, some 2.6 million state and local employees were covered by retirement plans. By 1978, the number had increased to 11.3 million.

In *The Making of the President, 1972,* Theodore H. White gives us one of his wonderful disquisitions on the meaning of our national statistics. After dealing with what the numbers tell us about the changing status of young Americans and women (among other groups), White turns to government workers.

> For none had [the 1960s] been a more prosperous decade than for those who worked in government—Federal, state and local. Not only had their salaries, pension rights and fringe benefits increased far faster than for those who worked in private employment. So, too, had their numbers. . . . Government workers lived better than most average Americans and they weighed heavily on the budgets of others; at the county, village and municipal level, their demand on taxes had risen by more than 100 percent.

White reminds us that this growth took place—whatever the politicians tell us now—because Americans wanted it.

> In the post-industrial world, Americans needed government more than ever—to clean their air and water, to preserve natural beauty, to balance the economy and provide jobs, to build roads and protect the streets, to educate the young and heal the sick.

But the fact remained (and remains) that the 1960s and 1970s witnessed the emergence as one of the newest of White's "constituency blocs" of the great cluster of workers at all levels of government.[3]

With growth has come power, and with power, assertiveness.

Back in 1919, the Boston police strike set the tone for our dealings with our public employees. The strike made Calvin Coolidge, of all people, a national hero. As governor of Massachusetts, Coolidge supposedly delayed calling in the State Guard until enough crime had occurred to turn the public against the striking police (who wanted to join the new AFL). Boston Police Commissioner Edwin U. Curtis then fired the strikers, and Coolidge backed him up with the celebrated dictum that there was "no right to strike against the public safety by anybody, anywhere, anytime."

For nearly half a century, the Coolidge attitude was the attitude of America. Thus, in 1947, in retaliation for a brief walkout of Buffalo schoolteachers, New York State passed the Condon-Wadlin Act. Under this law, if a public employee went out on strike, he was automatically dismissed. If he was rehired, he had to be placed on probation for five years, and for three years he forfeited all pay increases. So harsh was the act that it was rarely invoked. But its Draconian provisions were always at hand to intimidate the leaders and members of civil-service employees' associations. Quietly, these organizations gathered strength. In the mid-1960s, their time had come.

The turning point was the twelve-day strike Michael Quill's Transport Workers Union mounted against New York City in January 1966. Quill called out his people in defiance of a court injunction and, later, of a jail sentence for contempt of court. Before the strike was over, it had maimed the city and withered the reputation of its brand-new mayor, John V. Lindsay. The strikers gained a $61-million, 15 percent wage increase. The strike killed Mike Quill (felled by a heart attack two days after the strike began, he died at the end of January). But it also killed, as dead as mutton, the fiction that public employees were too loyal, too virtuous, or too timid to walk out, and that against "firmness" on the part of City Hall or the statehouse they couldn't win a strike.

Since 1966, the country has grown hardened to threats of noncooperation, mass resignations, and "sickouts" by public employees. Strikes, when they have been called, have proved traumatic. In 1968, New York City writhed once again, this time in the grip of a thirty-six-day teachers' strike that writer Martin Mayer called "the worst disaster" to hit New York in his lifetime, "much worse in its social effect than a major race riot." In 1970, a postal workers' strike, though only partly successful, screwed up mail delivery throughout the northeast. And after a decade of increasingly aggressive job actions including another severe New York City transit strike in 1980, came the 1980 Chicago firemen's strike, a sickening affair during which twenty-two Chicagoans died in poorly fought fires while negotiations were held up by both sides.

Trapped between a money-hungry police force, fire department, or teachers' union and an electorate in dire need of its cops, firemen, and teachers, a governor, county commissioner, or mayor truly does stand between "a rock and a hard place." If he gives in to the demands of the one group, the bill is apt to be a high one—all the higher because the other groups will soon demand at least as good a deal. But if he tries to stand firm, he places his constituents—which is to say, his political future—in hazard.

Very few of today's elected officials have the kind of courage that can stand up to, say, a three-week garbage strike. "God made the Hare and the Bengali," joked Rudyard Kipling's Kim about creatures timorous by nature. "What shame?" He might well have added the Politician to the list.

For political hares, life is much sweeter if they can talk public employees into going for fatter pensions instead of higher pay.* A pay hike, after all, is highly visible. So many dollars more per employee per month translates into the kind of money television newscasters know how to explain. *This* kind of money taxpayers, too, understand.

In contrast, a pension sweetener hardly shows. It can be, and usually is, worked out privily, not in the glare of publicity that generally surrounds formal collective-bargaining sessions. By the nature of pension funding, the cost of the increase will be spread over many future years. Given a cooperative actuary, changes in plan assumptions can bury without a trace all evidence of the increase. Indeed, actuarial cooperation may not even be necessary. Today, nearly 25 percent of all public pension plans are still being run without actuarial surveillance. Often, the costs of pension increases are not properly worked out. Often, they're not added to the costs already being carried.

The political leader who can sell a public employees' union a pension increase in lieu of a pay hike knows that the voters of his generation won't feel a thing. Besides, where voters see a salary increase as a shameless squandering of public funds, they're more likely to view a pension increase (if they find out about it) as an act of benevolence. Who could be against giving a little more money to a retired schoolteacher or cop?

To say the least, such attitudes hardly lead to well-designed, well-financed, soundly run pension systems. To chronicle the worst problems and abuses routine in public pensions today would take a separate book, one at least as thick as the 858-page *Pension Task Force Report* mentioned earlier. Here, it's possible to note only a bare handful of the most disturbing facts and examples. Let's begin with plan design.

Most private plans, as we've seen (page 19ff.), tie the benefit

---

* This is especially true since a pay increase almost always carries with it an increase in pension benefits, while the reverse is not the case.

to the individual's normal pay, excluding overtime. Most base the pension on the employee's "career-average" earnings, although many have turned to the more generous "final-average" figure to cushion the impact of inflation. But . . . more than one-quarter of all public pension plans recognize overtime in addition to regular pay. More than three-quarters use the costlier final-average pay base. Nearly one-fifth—over 1,200 plans—base pensions on the highest possible earnings figure, the rate of pay on the *final day* of work before retirement.

If you're in one of the 900-odd plans, most of them for policemen and firemen, that count overtime *and* use the last-day pay figure, you've got it made in the shade. If your lieutenant or captain will let you work two shifts on the day before you retire (and how can he refuse?), you can more than double your pension! And the rest of us look on in envy—and pay and pay at tax time.

In their 1979 study *Public Pension Plans,* Wharton Business School professors Howard E. Winklevoss and Dan M. McGill point out that such provisions are open invitations to abuse. "The most likely sources of abuse . . . are selective salary increases for those nearing retirement and . . . the concentration of overtime among those approaching retirement." Until 1976, New York City's pensions did count overtime and did base pensions on the final day's pay. (They still do, for everybody appointed before mid-1973.) According to Winklevoss and McGill, these practices "not only inflated the cost of the plans but produced pension benefits grossly in excess of those originally contemplated."[4]

A CBS News report (March 23, 1980) more than substantiated these findings. In a televised interview, New York City Police Commissioner Robert J. McGuire revealed that a precinct commander had permitted one of his men to build up more than $20,000 in overtime in one year and to elect early retirement—at 40 percent of total pay—based on earnings of more than $45,000. The commissioner said he favored "a change in regulations."

Policemen and firemen have it good in other ways, too.* For instance, in nine out of ten police and fire department plans, the

---

* To be fair, they also have it bad in some ways. For instance, in 12 percent of all police and fire plans, those who leave must forfeit all benefits including their own contributions.

standard retirement benefit is 50 percent of final pay. Some 650 of these plans (including among many other large ones that of New York City) make this benefit available to any participant, no matter what his age, after twenty years of service. A candidate can thus join a police force or fire department at, say twenty-two, work his way up to the $18,000 or $20,000 top pay-grade, then retire at forty-two on not less than $9,000 or $10,000 a year. Only, of course, he doesn't retire. He goes to work on full salary as a security guard or fire-insurance inspector—and in due course qualifies for a second pension.

In some places, the employee who retires from one department goes right to work for another branch of government, drawing his pension from his old job and his full pay for the new and getting ready to retire in earnest on two pensions. This is the "double dipping" that makes government service so delicious to thousands of employees.

About 65 percent of all police and firemen's plans feature immediate pensions, regardless of the individual's age or length of service, in case of a job-connected disability. For the cop hurt in a shootout or the fireman who breathes in too much smoke at a fire, such provisions are not unreasonable, although many planners strongly doubt whether the pension plan is the right vehicle for disability benefits. But as a final instance of how a worthwhile benefit can be turned into a giveaway, New York State's so-called heart bill is a classic. Every year in New York, the legislature is asked to renew an act that states that *any* heart ailment affecting a policeman or fireman is job related. This entitles the sufferer to an instant pension of 75 percent of pay for life. Exactly how the heart bill works out in practice is made clear by a story in the *New York Times* (February 9, 1977). The story explains how five New York City doctors, who did part-time duty as police surgeons, were able to retire under the heart bill with pensions of $21,000 to $25,600 a year while still continuing in private practice. (On February 10, Mayor Abraham D. Beame, upset by the story, ordered an investigation. Mayor Beame said he personally thought $20,000 a year would have been enough.)

If plan design seems out of kilter, public-pension-plan administration is often nightmarish. Most big plans are run by "retirement boards" that delegate their authority to paid administrators.

But hundreds of smaller state and local plans are administered directly by elected officeholders. According to the *Pension Task Force Report* (1978):

> In these smaller plans, city clerks, budget officers, even police chiefs may spend part of their time on pension plan administration and investment matters. Consultants, insurance agents, or insurance companies perform some or all of the administrative services for a majority of the smaller plans not having retirement boards.[5]

Private pension plans are managed almost entirely by the employers who sponsor the plans. But the *Pension Task Force Report* indicates that "employee representatives constitute a board majority in about one-third of all federal, state, and local systems." And yet, "employees have no representation in about 28 percent of the plans." The lack of consistency is striking. Should employees actually control their own plans, or should they have no say in them whatever? Our public officials obviously have no idea what the policy should be.

Large plans may have computerized their records and written down their procedures, but their administration will still be chaotic. One reason is that there are too many cooks. Says the *Task Force Report:*

> The time and attention of the plan administrator is demanded by legislative bodies, elected officials, various boards and commissions, employee representatives, and other special interests. . . . The ultimate authority . . . may reside in the mayor, the city council, the board of education, the police or fire commission, the governor, the state legislature, retirement or investment boards, the U.S. Congress, even collective bargaining agreements.[6]

Even when the purpose is to cut down the possibility of manipulation and abuse, "a maze of laws built up over time" may drive pension administrators crazy. Something like that seems to have happened in Michigan. There, officials charged with improving the administration of the state's 187 retirement plans wrote plaintively in May 1977: "Provisions . . . have become so vague and confusing that administrators . . . must select one of a variety of interpretations and hope they are right."

In smaller plans, administration sometimes becomes top heavy. Of the 5,788 state and local plans in being, nearly 80 percent have fewer than 100 active members. And 793 plans, or 13.7 percent, have fewer than 4 active members! Yet, some of these are supervised by whole boards of officials. In Illinois, for instance, a 1973 report revealed that a number of the 465 public pension plans had more members on their boards than participants.

More often, however, controls in smaller plans break down entirely. Appearing in September 1975 before the House Subcommittee on Labor Standards, William H. Wilcox of the Pennsylvania Department of Community Affairs testified that in his state some of the 1,413 public pension plans were being run without benefit of statute or even of written plan-document. Wilcox reported that when the police in one town learned that the chief of police was entitled to a bigger pension than his men, the officers took turns at the job to qualify themselves. Within six days, there were four different chiefs.

Absent from plans of all sizes are some of the most basic requirements of sound administration. One of these is the audit, the periodic independent review of plan operations and finances. The Pension Task Force discovered, first of all, that "about 4.6 percent of all state and local plans and 29.1 percent of all federal plans are not audited at all." Of plans with 1,000 or more members, 37 percent are not subject to annual audit. Furthermore, much of the auditing that is done is of doubtful adequacy.

For a pension plan to make any sense at all as an incentive to work harder or to remain loyal to an employer, its various benefits must be familiar to the participants. But in 18 percent of all federal plans and 21 percent of all state and local plans, participants are given *no description at all* of their plans (another 9 percent of federal and 26 percent of state and local plans will supply a description on request only). Only 36 percent of federal plans and 25 percent of state and local plans automatically tell their members what benefits have been built up for them. In nearly one out of four police and fire plans, the participants are *never* told what the buildup is.

As a result of their ignorance, employees who quit may "forfeit vested employee contributions or other benefits." A 1976 report of the New Jersey State Legislature suggests that this state's plans "have accumulated millions of dollars in unclaimed benefits." At the federal level, the General Accounting Office, the watchdog agency of Congress, as far back as 1972 reported that the Civil Service Retirement System, by far the biggest of the federal plans, had lost track of some 338,000 retired members whose unclaimed benefits were worth $26 million.

But the gravest problems of all occur in the crucial area of plan finance. Here the stakes are immense. The assets of the nation's public pension plans are growing at the rate of about 13 percent a year. In 1979, they were worth approximately $220 billion. This huge sum, interestingly, was more than two-thirds of the $321 billion held by private plans, even though the public plans cover only one-third as many employees. (The main reason is that the retired public employee gets average benefits that are more than 70 percent higher than those paid to the private-sector employee.)

There's something rotten about virtually every aspect of the management of public pension reserves. We can start with the incredible finding of the Pension Task Force that despite the vastness of these reserves, "17 percent of all public pension plans are still found to be operated on a pay-as-you-go basis." That is, *no* reserves have been set up to cover the accumulated past-service liabilities (see pages 55–56). This in turn means two things. First, in such plans no funds are available to secure the growing pension rights of plan members. Second, as the number of retired persons mounts, the cost to pay-as-you-go will begin to spiral upward. The *Task Force Report* indicates that eventually, under the pay-as-you-go method, pension costs of 50 percent or even 75 percent of payroll will be required.

> Ultimately, the advocates of pay-as-you-go financing [argue that] the unlimited power of government to tax serves as an adequate guarantee of such payments.

After a somber look at this argument, the authors of the report reject it. In the long run, they say, state and local governments "can and will renege on . . . pension commitments" when pension costs "threaten the government unit's fiscal stability."[7] This is the scenario for a horror movie: Cops go berserk when the mayor tells them they're not going to collect the pensions the politicians promised them.

The *Task Force Report* winds up its remarks on pay-as-you-go with a comment that every reader of this book, I'm sure, will want to cheer. "The ability to tax is in fact limited by the ability and willingness of the citizen to pay."

Reserve funds have been set up for most public plans. How adequate are they? That is what actuaries are hired to figure out; yet, an astonishing 24 percent of all public plans have either *never* had an actuarial valuation or have had none performed during the past ten years. How can their managers know whether there's enough money in the kitty to cover current plan liabilities? They can't.

Forty-two percent of all public plans do have reserves but don't build them up on an actuarially sound basis. This doesn't always mean that such plans have too little money. Sometimes they have too much. In Alabama and Arkansas, for instance, local- and state-police pensions are funded in part out of the proceeds of traffic fines. Sometimes, the speed traps and the radar just don't thrive. But there are periods when so much money flows in from fines that a glut of cash results: more than enough cash to cover current pension outlays.

The use of an actuary and of actuarially designed assumptions and funding methods is clearly a step in the right direction. But the mere presence of an actuary is no guarantee at all that public plans are secure. In New York City, the devices politicians use to get around bothersome actuarial requirements are as noisome as overripe Limburger. One ploy is to make the required pension contributions for a given year not in that year, but two years later. "Ostensibly," says Professor Damodar Gujarati, "the reason for this lag is that it facilitates [administration]. The real reason is financial: it is a gimmick to avoid paying the contribution in the current fiscal year."[8] An even simpler gimmick is not to pay at all. According to a recent report of the Mayor's Management Advisory Council and the New York State Insurance Department, nearly one-fifth of the combined assets of the city's five major pension plans is "accrued but unpaid city contributions": money the city owes but has yet to come up with.

Although New York City's politicians lead the pack in the cool nerve they display toward evading pension obligations, Gotham is by no means unique. In Illinois and Washington, financial problems have forced cuts in pension contributions to levels very far below those the actuaries deem safe and the law requires. Indeed, the Pension Task Force terms such underfunding a "coast-to-coast phenomenon." In over 15 percent of all large plans (those with at least 1,000 members), actual contributions were 20 percent *or more* below what their actuaries were saying they should be. Evidently, political leaders across the country are shrugging their shoulders, shortchanging the pension cash drawer, and hoping not to get caught.

In public as in private plans, a favorite way of keeping current costs down is to juggle the actuarial assumptions. As we've seen, plan assumptions must change—gradually—to reflect what actually happens in such areas as investment earnings, employee turnover, compensation, disability, and mortality. Otherwise, the control of pension costs can go haywire. Manipulating assumptions to make a federal, state, or city budget look better is a risky practice. Nevertheless, it appears to be widespread. Says the *Pension Task Force Report:* "The fact that some plans [do so] renders meaningless any broad-brush attempt to characterize 'actuarial funding' as being synonymous with 'adequate funding.' "

Another trouble spot, and quite possibly the most sensitive one of all, is investment. Consider the possibilities: officials who may or may not know anything about investment mechanics or pension investment are entrusted with scores of millions of dollars to invest over long periods. At every stage of the process, opportunities abound for these officials to pocket something extra, and almost no way exists for outsiders to uncover the chicanery. Legislatures and city councils can—and do—set up elaborate systems of financial control. But who can control a gift of stock that's on its way up, let alone a midnight visit to an official's home with a bagful of money?

In his study of public-employee pension-fund-asset management, Louis Kohlmeier uncovered the classic case of investment double-dealing in the experience of the Albany, Georgia, public pension fund. Between 1961 and 1972, the bank handling the city's pension money earned an annual investment return of 1.1 percent. The chairman of the pension board was a director of the bank. When a city financial official leaked the ridiculously low figure and demanded an investigation, the irate board chairman called his action "politically motivated." Meanwhile, Albany's actuarial consultant had set the plan's interest assumption at 8 percent per year. The city fired the bank and has spent the last eight years trying to make up the shortfall.

To minimize the chances of this sort of dishonesty, many cities and states have turned to major banks and asset-management firms. But most have not. More than twenty states, and hundreds of county and municipal governments, rely entirely on "internal administration" in the investment of their pension funds. One state that does so is Alabama. In an interview in the trade journal *Pensions and Investments* (October 25, 1976), Dr. David G. Bronner, treasurer of the then $217-million (now $1.8 billion) Alabama Employees' Retirement System, reported on the bribes being offered to him by brokers eager for his investment business. In blunt terms, Dr. Bronner pointed out how vulnerable he and officials like him were to corruption:

> [There are] absolutely no policy guidelines for the person in my position. There are no policies on such things as self-dealing, dealing in hot issues. . . . There is no policy requiring disclosure of any transactions I make for my personal account, no disclosure of who loans are made to [by the pension fund] and any relationship the person in my position may have with those parties.

It's not that public-sector pension investment is universally dishonest—far from it. But in the absence of such safeguards as audits and accurate records, there's no way of knowing what does in fact go on.

Then, too, without written guidelines, deciding who's to blame for bad or crooked investment management—and trying to recover the money—becomes difficult or even impossible. Yet, the Pension Task Force discovered that, in 1975, twenty-two of the fifty states had *no* written rules on how state pension funds should be invested. On the twenty-two-state list were most of the southern states and many western states; lest the cynic laugh too soon, so also were such supposed models of good state government as California, Iowa, and Vermont.

Like administration in general, investment-making is occasionally hampered by too much rather than too little control. One of the problems is legislation (often lobbied into being by local financial interests) requiring the use of "home team" investment specialists. Louis Kohlmeier picks out such provincialism as a serious issue:

> One of the most persistent conflict-of-interest situations results from ... hiring local brokers, bankers and investment advisors, and the practice of investing in local securities, even though better—or lower-cost—services and higher-yielding investments may well be available outside local boundaries.[9]

Citing Pennsylvania, Illinois, and New Jersey as examples, the Pension Task Force found that almost one-fifth of all big public plans could hire as investment counselors only those firms with in-state or local offices. For buying and selling securities, nearly "two-thirds of *all* governmental plans were . . . required to use local or in-state brokerage firms."

In 1977, the U.S. Census Bureau discovered that the retirement system of Revere, Massachusetts, had placed 59 percent of its funds in state and local government bonds. Jersey City, New Jersey, had done the same thing with 35 percent of its pension money. These bonds are for people in high tax brackets. Because the income is tax exempt, their yield is lower than that of corporate bonds. Nevertheless, the rich who buy them very often come out ahead. Why should a pension fund, with no taxes to pay, put money into tax-exempt securities? Robert Tilove, author of an authoritative Twentieth Century Fund study of public pension plans, says simply that the practice is, "with rare exceptions, senseless."

The Pension Task Force conducted its research during the mid-1970s and brought out its report in 1978. Are its findings still valid in the early 1980s? Asked this question, Task Force head Russ Mueller permits himself a rare grin. "We gathered so much information," he says happily, "that the interest groups like the Governors' Conference and the National League of Cities really couldn't say much. They sort of wish the report would go away. But all they can do is come out and say, 'Okay, we've got problems, we've got problems.' And now, they've all got task forces of their own to work on their problems. Sure, there have been some changes. But nothing substantial has changed."

Isn't there one state or city or hamlet that has dealt wisely and honestly with its pension plans, one shining example in a naughty world? Again, Russ Mueller grins. This time, you'd swear you'd spotted something almost wolfish in the grin—except that Mueller's blond good looks seem too innocent. "My friend," says the man who has probably examined more public pension plans than anyone else in the world, "I can't give you a historical example where things went well. Not a single one."

In classic westerns, there's often a scene in which the poor nester, his fences smashed, his crops flattened, rides into town to the sheriff's office to seek justice. The sheriff listens politely. But as he listens, his hand is stealthily sliding open his desk drawer to get at the .44 inside. The camera shows you what the nester has yet to find out: that the sheriff himself is one of the badmen.

What does the Congress of the United States do about pensions for its members? To find out things about Congress, you call the Capitol. In due course, if you start on the House side, you reach the office of the Sergeant at Arms. "Well," a soft-spoken voice told me, "members of Congress are covered by the federal Civil Service Retirement System, just like everybody else. There's no special plan just for members." I thanked my informant and hung up, reassured. Not until I was much deeper into my research did I discover that senators and representatives—and the 18,019 men and women who work for them, at home and in Washington— are indeed covered by the Civil Service Retirement System. But within this system, not everyone is treated "just like everybody else." As George Orwell has it in *Animal Farm:* "Some are more equal than others."

In 1937, congressional employees, who previously had to rely on the capricious generosity of the individual senators and representatives they worked for, were given the right to join the Civil Service Retirement System. But not until 1946 did the members of Congress themselves follow their aides, staff assistants, and clerks into the CSRS. When they did so, moreover, they quietly made sure that the system would take very good care of them. For members of Congress, pensions were figured on the basis of 2.5 percent of salary, *versus* 1.5 percent for everybody else. And members voted themselves the right to retire at sixty-two, on full pension, after just six years of congressional service. This was done, explained the legislative history of the act, "in recognition of the arduous labors imposed on all Members."

In 1954, congressional employees (as well as congressmen) were granted the right to use the special 2.5 percent rate in figuring their retirement benefits. Congress allowed itself a little something more: the right to retire at sixty, on a slightly reduced pension, after ten years of service. Everybody else in the CSRS needed thirty years of service to retire early. But a committee report on the change stated that "the benefits provided were not any more liberal than the comparable present retirement provisions for other Federal employees."

Two years later, Congress changed the rules again, to allow both members *and* employees to retire on full pension at sixty-two, after only five years of service. Members but *not* employees who had served for ten years or more could retire on full pensions at sixty. And congressmen also voted in 1956 to pay an immediate pension to the widows or widowers of deceased members; this would equal 50 percent of what the member would have received at sixty-two had he or she lived. For everybody else in the CSRS, "survivor benefits" consisted of a return of the dead employee's own contributions.

In 1960, Congress voted itself an even juicier pension arrangement. Now, any member fifty or older who is "separated from service other than by resignation or expulsion after service in nine Congresses"—they might as well have said, "any senator who serves three terms, then loses an election"—can draw an immediate pension. (If the member is younger than sixty, the pension will be somewhat smaller than it would have been if he were sixty or older.) What's more, after twenty years of federal service, ten or more of which have been in Congress, a congressman who leaves for *any* reason, including expulsion, can get a pension beginning when he's fifty.

Jolliest of all, they souped up their own pension formula. Congressmen and their employees can now apply the special 2.5 percent rate to their highest-average salaries.* They can count

* Originally, to the average of the five highest years' earnings. But since 1969, to that of the three highest years' earnings, an even more liberal rule.

military and congressional service at this high rate. Other government service also counts, at rates higher than those for all other
CSRS members.

What does all of this mean in terms of hard cash? A simple example will illustrate. Let's consider the case of Congressman Joe
Blowhard, who was forty-eight in 1980. After college, Joe served
for three years in the army. Then, he went to law school, got his
degree, came to Washington and went to work for $20,000 a year
as staff counsel to a presidential commission. At thirty-five, Joe
ran for Congress from his home district, whipped the senile incumbent, and has been in the House ever since.

If he keeps his seat until he's sixty, Joe will retire at that age
on a pension of $49,700.28 a year. In contrast, a noncongressional
civil servant with a service record and earnings exactly comparable would retire on a yearly pension of $26,506.82. To repeat:
Some are more equal than others.

Nobody would argue that congressmen should be denied adequate pensions. Indeed, alongside the retirement benefits the senior executives of big American companies have carved out for
themselves, congressional pension behavior seems almost dainty.
To pick out just a few examples:* John D. deButts, board chairman of AT&T, was scheduled to retire in 1980 on a pension of
$300,000 a year. Frank T. Cary, IBM's board chairman, also re-
tired in 1980, on $120,000 a year. When John F. McGillicuddy
of Manufacturers Hanover Trust steps down, he'll get at least
$120,400 a year. C. B. Branch, the chief executive officer of Dow
Chemical, will receive $278,000 a year at his retirement, and a
dozen other Dow executives are in line for six-figure pensions.

Most delectable of all is the feast ITT had ready for Harold S.
Geneen when he retired at the end of 1979. Geneen receives, in
addition to a pension of $243,097, consulting fees of $450,000 in
1980 and $250,000 a year through 1985. He also gets higher life
insurance and disability coverage, office space, security protection, secretarial aid, and limousine service. In comparison, congressmen have barely dipped their snouts into the benefit trough.

Still, Congress doesn't really treat itself "just like everybody
else" in federal employment, and it's wrong to pretend that it

---

* From a February 1978 analysis in *Dun's Review* and from a report (April 2,
1980) in the *New York Times.*

does. Few top executives can qualify for their pensions, however huge, as congressmen do for theirs, after only five years of service. (Harold Geneen, for example, held his ITT chairmanship for 21 years.) Above all, Congress will find it hard to press for the desperately needed reform of public pension systems when its own system is so open to "adjustment" in its own favor.

Let's close this survey of the pensions our public servants receive with a quick glance at the very top of the greasy pole, the presidency. As we've already noted, George Washington never received a pension from his grateful country. Nor, for 163 years, did any of his successors in the presidency. Dwight D. Eisenhower, when he left office in 1960, became the first president of the United States to benefit from the Presidential Retirement System that Congress set up in 1958. According to the slightly confused prose of a 1978 General Accounting Office report on federal retirement systems, Congress was not worrying about poverty.

> A Senate report on proposed legislation to establish the Presidents' retirement system recognized there are many ways in which a former President can earn a large income but maintained that, by providing a retirement benefit, former Presidents could be expected not to engage in any business which would demean the office of President.[10]

Thus, a retired president now gets an immediate pension equal to the salary of a cabinet-level department secretary: in 1980, $69,630 a year. Every time this Level 1 Civil Service salary goes up—or, what has never happened, down—the income of any presidential retiree changes automatically. The legal right to the pension is vested in the individual at once when he assumes office. (The fact would seem to make moot all the arguments about whether Richard M. Nixon, if he were impeached and convicted, could keep his pension.) The income is suspended if the former president takes a job, for other than a nominal salary, with either the federal government or the District of Columbia. But there's no restriction on earnings from other sources.

The Presidential Retirement System also provides a survivor benefit for the widows of former presidents, a modest life income of $20,000 a year. The widow forfeits the pension if she remarries before reaching sixty or if she accepts any other federally mandated pension, including—presumably—Social Security.

Whatever we may find to say about public pensions in America, and there's plenty to say, it's hard to criticize what we do for those we elect to our highest office. Presidents may be the most powerful individuals in the world. But unless things change dramatically, no president will get rich from his pension.

★ 6 ★

Social Security:
The Barons of Benevolence

It's amazing how quickly we forget.

Not much more than a generation ago, everybody worked at least half a day on Saturdays. Paid holidays? You got Thanksgiving, Christmas, New Year's Day, Decoration Day, and the Fourth of July. Unless you were a schoolteacher (or the boss), you were allowed one week's paid vacation each year until you'd been on the job for perhaps twenty years. Then, depending on the whim of the boss, you might or might not get a second week. If you wanted to go to night school to improve yourself, or if your child needed an operation, *you* came up with the cash.

Nobody found anything odd, much less unjust, about such arrangements. This was the way things were in the 1920s, 1930s, and early 1940s. The best summary I've heard of the work ethic of those times came from an expert, my father, who, like so many others, lived through them to prosper later. "Back then," he used to say, with no discernible nostalgia whatever, "if you did a wonderful job, the company had a wonderful fringe benefit for you. They let you keep your job."

One other thing. When you got too old or too sick to work, you retired. You lived on whatever you'd managed to save, and on the kindness of your children or other relatives, until you died. You could expect to die within a very few years. If you had no savings and no one to take you in, you went—literally—to the poorhouse or the county old-folks' home.

This was the sociological backdrop against which the bleak drama of Depression unemployment was enacted. We forget it because, naturally enough, we want to forget what happened to millions of Americans during those years. We forget, too, what the visionaries and the demagogues of the day had in mind for the old and the poor. Who now remembers novelist Upton Sinclair's plan to End Poverty In California (EPIC) via state socialism? Or even the much grander scheme advanced by retired California physician Francis E. Townsend? The "Townsend Old Age Revolving Pension Plan" was very simple. Every U.S. citizen over sixty would be given a pension of $200 a month. The only proviso was that the recipient had to spend the money within thirty days. A 2 percent national sales tax would cover the cost of the plan. The increased purchasing power thus injected into the economy would automatically solve not only the financial problems of the aged but the unemployment problem as well.

We forget ... but in the mid-1930s, over 10 million people signed Townsend petitions, joined Townsend Clubs, and subscribed to *The Townsend Weekly.**

Then there was Rev. Charles Coughlin, the celebrated "radio priest" of Detroit. Father Coughlin founded the "National Union for Social Justice" to crusade for a silver-backed currency (shades of William Jennings Bryan!), for nationalizing industry, and for saving the working man from "the vested interests." Until the Social Justice movement collapsed in a welter of Hitlerite rhetoric and anti-Semitism and his religious superiors ordered the radio priest off the air, Father Coughlin, too, had millions of followers.

And what of Senator Huey P. Long of Louisiana, who pro-

---

* Dr. Townsend lost much of his personal popularity after he refused to answer the questions posed by a congressional investigating committee and was declared in contempt of Congress (only President Roosevelt's pardon saved Townsend from a jail sentence). But Townsendism as a movement went on and in fact still survives.

claimed over the radio on February 23, 1934, his plan to "Share Our Wealth"? Long's proposal involved taxing "the rich" to give everybody a $5,000 homestead, a car, a radio, a washing machine, and much more. To enlist converts under the SOW banner, the Kingfish hired a flamboyant, thirty-year-old Disciples of Christ preacher named Gerald L. K. Smith. Smith, who later became the doyen of America's white supremacists, toured the towns and hamlets of the Delta South with his master's message. "Let's pull down these huge piles of gold until there shall be a real job," he would shout. "Not a little old sow-belly, black-eyed pea job but a real spending money, beefsteak and gravy, Chevrolet, Ford in the garage, new suit, Thomas Jefferson, Jesus Christ, red, white, and blue job for every man!" According to T. Harry Williams's brilliant biography of Huey Long[1] (from which the Smith quotation also comes), within eighteen months there were 27,431 Share Our Wealth clubs, with a total membership of 4.7 million.

Out of this maelstrom of Depression helplessness, fumbling humanitarianism, and political discontent, Social Security was born.

The story has been told many times—and with varying degrees of accuracy—of how Franklin D. Roosevelt took unto himself and the Democratic party the cause of federal social legislation. Why Roosevelt did so has never been entirely clear. Was he what his wife termed him—"a very simple Christian" with a Christian's desire to end poverty and suffering? Or was he merely an astute politician with his mind on the 1936 election, essentially a conservative whose hand was forced by populists like Coughlin and Long? Probably, of course, he was both. But the key fact is that Roosevelt, for all his talk about a "cradle-to-grave" system that "Mose Smith, my farm manager" would understand, was too shrewd merely to obey his own instincts. Dr. Townsend claimed divine inspiration for his plan. Huey Long reportedly put together the Share Our Wealth program at three o'clock one morning in his bedroom in Washington's Mayflower Hotel. Roosevelt did something different. In June 1934, he set up the Committee on Economic Security, put his key cabinet officials on it, and staffed it with experts in economics, the social sciences, and public administration. The triumvirate of Roosevelt himself, Harry L. Hopkins, and Secretary of Labor Frances Perkins supplied the political muscle. But it was the committee staff that slaved to make sure Social Security was neither a visionary fantasy nor a politician's vote-getting sham, but a carefully wrought, durable reality.

From the start, opposition was intense. In April 1935, the Republicans on the House Ways and Means Committee voted to a man against Roosevelt's economic security bill. Their reasons:

> [Its old-age provisions] impose a crushing burden upon industry and upon labor.
>
> They establish a bureaucracy in the field of insurance in competition with private business.
>
> They destroy old-age retirement systems set up by private industry . . .

Almost as an afterthought, the Republicans declared that Social Security was unconstitutional.

Arthur J. Altmeyer, the Wisconsin-born administrative wizard who soon became chairman of the Social Security Board, writes that at least one of these Republicans favored the Townsend Plan. "It seemed incongruous," Altmeyer says,

> that a conservative should consider a universal pension plan paying a large, flat amount irrespective of need, to be less of a threat to our existing institutions than a contributory social insurance system paying benefits related to wage loss.[2]

The wry remark underscores a key truth. From Roosevelt down, the original architects of Social Security considered themselves conservative, not radical, in their aims. They had in mind a pension system of three parts. The "floor" of the system was Social Security itself. Its benefits, like those of private retirement plans, were to be related to earnings and length of service. Again, exactly as in private plans, the benefits were to flow from a trust fund supported by contributions from both employers and employees. This fund would be invested in government securities. The whole plan would be monitored by actuaries and run on a nonpolitical basis. Even its administrative budget, financed like the benefits themselves via a tax on payrolls, would be separate from those of all other government departments.

The individual's own savings would provide the second layer of retirement protection. (At first, the planners wanted to offer low-cost government annuities to encourage people to save for retirement. The life insurance industry, scared by the idea, succeeded in lobbying the annuity provision out of the bill.)

Only for those whose Social Security and savings would be inadequate to supply food, clothing, and shelter was a third layer proposed: public assistance or "welfare" benefits. These were to be federally financed but administered by the states.

As for the management of Social Security, a three-man board was to handle decision making and policy. The board was dissolved in 1946 as too cumbersome, and a single commissioner has since served as chief executive officer of Social Security. At the risk of getting ahead of our story, we should meet here some of those who from the start have played the key roles in management. For sixteen years, from 1937 to 1953, the remarkable Arthur Altmeyer held the job of commissioner. Taking over from Altmeyer, in fact and philosophy if not in name, was the equally remarkable Robert M. Ball, who ran Social Security at first as deputy director of the Bureau of Old Age and Survivors Insurance and then, from 1962 to 1973, as commissioner. Robert J. Myers, who took over as chief actuary when W. Rulon Williamson, the first to hold the post, resigned in 1949, proved brilliant at explaining the program's complexities to its congressional overseers. Even after Myers resigned in 1970, he remained (and remains) a kind of ayatollah in exile, a major figure to be consulted on Social Security policy issues.*

Its designers may have thought Social Security a conservative program, but its opponents trembled as if Armageddon had arrived. During the floor debate in the House, Congressman John Taber of New York rose in fury. "Never in the history of the world," he asserted, "has any measure been brought here so insidiously designed as to prevent business recovery, to enslave workers, and to prevent any possibility of the employers' providing work for the people." Another Republican congressman warned, "The lash of the dictator will be felt and twenty-five million free Americans will for the first time submit themselves to a fingerprint test."

---

* For this thumbnail sketch of some of Social Security's leaders, and for much else, I am indebted to Martha Derthick's brilliant study *Policymaking for Social Security* (1979). We'll hear more from Miss Derthick later in this chapter.

In the Senate, the attackers were less devoid of humor. "Now, Miss Perkins," the blind Senator Gore of Oklahoma asked the Secretary of Labor, "wouldn't you agree that there is a teeny-weeny bit of socialism in your program?"

Despite all of the invective and the grim jesting, the House passed the bill by a vote of 371 to 33, and the Senate voted 77 to 6 in its favor. Two months later, on August 14, 1935, the Social Security Act became law.

Having breathed life into Social Security, Congress sometimes seems to have spent the next forty-five years trying to cripple or dismantle what it had created.

Arthur Altmeyer, whose poker face conceals a dry wit and a long, long memory, recalls that the first assaults on the system were aimed at its hiring practices. Even though Social Security jobs were made subject to civil service rules, Depression-era congressmen saw in the new agency a choice source of patronage. Fred M. Vinson of Kentucky, the powerful chairman of the House Ways and Means Committee (and later chief justice of the U.S. Supreme Court), was a chief offender. At one point, when Altmeyer was being stubborn about hiring an unqualified Vinson protégé, "Mr. Vinson lost his temper, pushed me against a wall, shook his fist at me, and shouted in emphatic expletives that he also had a conscience!"

Later, a story made the rounds that the Social Security Board was appointing "too damned many New York Jews." Says Altmeyer:

> [Vinson] also told me this in more kindly and diplomatic language, saying that he had a very high regard for "members of your race" but that he and his associates were disturbed at the large number the Board was hiring. He was quite disturbed to learn that I was not, in fact, Jewish.[3]

The probable basis for the story was that Wilbur J. Cohen, whom Altmeyer had hired as a special assistant, was Jewish.

Much more important—and still at issue today—was the question of the Social Security "reserve fund." Roosevelt had always thought of the old-age provisions of Social Security as a kind of personal retirement-insurance policy for the worker. That is, the worker's own contributions, together with those of his employer (or employers) were supposed to provide enough money to cover the full cost of the retirement benefit. While this couldn't be true for those retiring during the early years of Social Security, it could be true later on. Contribution levels had deliberately been set high enough to allow this to happen. The magic date was 1980. By then, the actuaries estimated, the reserve fund would have reached $47 billion, a sum sufficiently big that the interest it earned, plus inflowing contributions, would cover the full cost of future benefits.

But for years, while the reserve was building up, annual Social Security contributions would add up to more than the annual cost of Social Security benefits. These "profits," as well as the unprecedented size of the reserve itself (in 1938, the entire national debt was only $25 billion), made Congress very nervous. Meanwhile, Frances Perkins, Arthur Altmeyer, and their allies, with the cautious support of the president, were trying to liberalize the whole of the program. Committees were formed and reports were drafted; finally, a bargain was struck. In August 1939, Congress in its wisdom did several things to Social Security. It increased the benefits and expanded the coverage. It moved up the day when retirement payments could be claimed. But it held to the $3,000 ceiling on earnings subject to Social Security taxes.

These moves assured that the buildup of reserves would take place much more slowly. The reserve, indeed, was reduced to the status of a contingency fund. Thus, four years after Social Security began, Congress and the administration together had quietly put aside the Rooseveltian goal of a fully funded old-age "insurance policy" for working Americans.

Not until 1950 were further major changes made in Social Security. But throughout the 1940s and beyond, one issue in particular remained alive: the old Townsend Plan idea of a fixed pension for everybody.

Perhaps because the flat-benefit system looks so simple and efficient, it has an almost irresistible appeal to populists, radicals of the right, and other believers in simple answers to hard questions. Under such a system, all the government has to do is send every oldster a check for X dollars each month. The pettifogging rules and formulas for deciding who gets what can be swept aside. And the flat-benefit pension scheme has another undeniable advantage.

In any system that gears benefits to earnings and service, there will always be a few luckless souls—a very few—who earn one penny less than the minimum or quit work one day too soon, and so lose out. A flat-benefit pension puts an end to such inequities.

But . . . what amount should X dollars be?

This one question exposes the fatal flaw in Townsendite thinking. For, whatever the amount, the pension that seems bountiful to some Americans is going to seem inadequate to others. Those others, just as hardworking and conscientious as their neighbors, will feel deprived, even cheated. In the nature of things, they'll apply to Congress for an increase in the benefit and vote for those candidates who promise to oblige. (Increases in the taxes that cover the cost will be less popular!) In the end, divorcing pensions entirely from individual need transforms them from instruments of social policy into playthings of politics.

Its drawbacks notwithstanding, Townsendism and its well-organized supporters haunted the Social Security Board for many years. Even those politicians who knew better, Democrat as well as Republican, flirted with the universal pension idea. Thus, in Senate Finance Committee hearings held in January 1950, no less a personage than Senator Robert A. Taft asked Arthur Altmeyer: "What would you think of the suggestion that we simply put everybody under the Federal old-age and survivors insurance at a minimum rate?" Altmeyer's answer was: "First, you have a political question. It really is not a technical question. It is a political question of what this flat amount is going to be. You suggest $25. Somebody else may suggest $50. Somebody else may suggest $100." In a year that saw Social Security vastly broadened and liberalized, Taft (a believer in Social Security) did not pursue the argument. But others were to do so.

In November 1952, a few days after Eisenhower's election as president, the U.S. Chamber of Commerce voted sixteen to one in favor of a "single, all-inclusive system, on a pay-as-you-go basis, providing a basic layer of social security benefits to all the retired aged." The shrewdly worded proposal was Townsendism in disguise. Its advocates were strongly represented in the celebrated "Hobby Lobby," the group Mrs. Oveta Culp Hobby, the then-new Federal Security Administrator, put together to study Social Security. Only strenuous efforts by organized labor and other friends of the existing system kept the Hobby Lobby from trying to sell Eisenhower on a Townsend-style universal flat pension.

One year later, Carl T. Curtis, congressman (and later senator) from Nebraska, launched an all-out attack on Social Security. The staff director of Curtis's special House subcommittee was the coauthor of a Townsendite book. Other staff members were former Chamber of Commerce employees. Earlier, Curtis had startled his House colleagues and everyone else by denouncing Oveta Culp Hobby. "It is hard to believe that Mrs. Hobby has been insincere in her statements about improving Social Security," Curtis told the press, "but the fact remains that her department [Health, Education, and Welfare] is not cooperating." In November 1953, Curtis took on Arthur Altmeyer, who had recently retired as commissioner for Social Security.

Their encounter was long and rancorous, but it did bring out one significant issue. Curtis, the Townsendite, pressed Altmeyer to justify his use of the term *insurance* in describing Social Security. Curtis wanted the word to mean something like what it means in law: a contractual agreement between the individual and an insurance company, whereby the latter, in return for premium payments, binds itself to make good a specified financial loss. Without such a contract, Curtis insisted, those covered under Social Security had no true right to their benefits. At any time, the government might take them away.

Curtis's populist mistrustfulness infuriated Altmeyer, who had spent a lifetime making government both honest and strong. Of course Social Security was "insurance," he told Curtis over and over. It was "social insurance," part of the contract every modern society makes with its members and articulates through its laws.

> I think that the statutory right is far stronger than a contractual right under some insurance companies, for the very reason that you have a responsible legislative body, the Congress. . . . You have at the present time about 90 million people who have accumulated wage credits. Now, it is inconceivable to me that the Congress of the United States would ever think of taking action to prejudice their rights.[4]

Curtis was no match in debate for Arthur Altmeyer. A Democrat on the subcommittee, enjoying the chairman's discomfiture, asked him: "What's wrong? Have you a porcupine by the tail and don't know what to do with him?"

And yet, Curtis did have a point to make, although he himself never made it.

Insurance, as well as being a matter of contract, is a matter of faith. People did—many still do—think of Social Security as insurance, with their contributions and those of their employers as the premiums that, over the years, cover the cost of their benefits. For this reason, they trusted Social Security.

Arthur Altmeyer himself had endorsed full funding of Social Security. Better than anyone, he knew that the move away from full funding in 1939 had ended Social Security's brief term as a true insurance program. This, he was certain, would never affect the payment of benefits: The country, having once committed itself to the program, would never turn back. Nevertheless, Altmeyer's persistence in labeling Social Security "insurance" has, I suspect, misled many Americans straight into the ditch of disillusionment. Ironically, the staunchest defender of Social Security paved the way for Curtis and others to undermine confidence in Social Security by their claim—absurd but telling—that because Social Security isn't insurance, it isn't sound.

In the 1950s, this claim disturbed no one except the dwindling band of Townsendites. Curtis himself did introduce a bill calling for a universal forty-five-dollar-a-month pension, but it went nowhere. President Eisenhower came out firmly in support of the system as it stood. In January 1954, he called Social Security "the cornerstone of the Government's program to promote the economic security of the individual." Rather than sponsoring the radical changes favored by his party's right wing, Eisenhower threw his prestige behind further liberalizations. Eisenhower, the nonpolitician, was much too astute politically to tamper with a program Americans had come to love. It's worthy of note that such innovations as disability payments and the beginnings of Medicare were added to Social Security during the eight happy years of Eisenhower's presidential reign.

It was left to another time, and to a very different Republican, to mount the next challenge to Social Security.

Barry Goldwater's position on Social Security, as he began his campaign for the presidency in 1964, seemed roughly like that of the southern senator in the celebrated story about the school desegregation crisis. "Son," this stalwart is supposed to have drawled to a reporter, "I surely don't favor this here segregation, not at all."

"What's that, Senator?" said the startled journalist. "Are you trying to tell me you favor integration?"

"Naw, son," the lawmaker growled, "I believes in *slavery.*"

Barry Goldwater, contrary to legend, never said in so many words that he was against Social Security. What he did say, in Concord, New Hampshire, on January 6, 1964, was: "I would like to suggest one change, that Social Security be made voluntary, that if a person can provide better for himself, let him do it." Now, as Goldwater must have known, a voluntary Social Security System would be an actuary's nightmare. If people could refuse to join, or could drop out whenever they chose, for whatever private reason, Social Security as we know it would fall apart.

Politically, Goldwater's remark was an act of *hara-kiri.* The next day's *Concord Monitor* headlined it: "GOLDWATER SETS GOALS: END SOCIAL SECURITY." Within hours, the 100 million Social Security enrollees and beneficiaries had heard the word. Later, in Chicago, Goldwater's fellow-Republican and fellow-conservative William Scranton would tell an audience: "This man has no part of the heritage of a true conservative. . . . Would Bob Taft destroy Social Security?" Later still, Goldwater's people got together an official statement affirming the Senator's support of the system. "I favor a sound Social Security System," it read,

> and I want to see it strengthened. I want to see every participant receive all the benefits this system provides. And I want to see these benefits paid in dollars with real purchasing power.

But by then it was too late. Goldwater's self-inflicted wound could not be healed.[5]

A dozen years later, Goldwater was still crying out that he'd been wronged. His 1976 book *The Coming Breakpoint* contains a chapter called "The Social Security Mess." It opens with characteristic Goldwater restraint. "Social Security has given the gnomes, the money manipulators of Washington, an almost life-and-death power over millions of Americans." After some anticlimactic grumbling, Goldwater flatly states, "Of course, the charge that I wanted to abolish Social Security [in 1964] had no basis in fact." He next talks about the need for "major changes," giving no specifics, and then, astonishingly, says:

> We might even see the day—and not too far off—when this country will have no Social Security program at all. I believe ways and means could be found to close out this program without injuring a single person and without cheating a single worker who has paid into it.[6]

Perhaps the Senator will admit that *now* he wants to abolish Social Security.

In fact, in 1976 as in 1964, Goldwater, no less than Carl Curtis and Francis Townsend and Huey Long and Ronald Reagan,* was trying to deliver a message to America. He was trying to say that Social Security, in some way that the heat of a political campaign and the pressure of writing a book made impossible to clarify, was a wrongly conceived system that is bad for Americans. Let it not be forgotten that Barry Goldwater's grandfather, from a standing start as a peddler, built the finest retail business in Arizona and one of the best in the country. For the grandson of Big Mike Goldwater, it's axiomatic that people should *want* to provide for themselves and their families. If they don't want to, they're wrong or weak or wicked. But government should not, must not, cozen them into doing that which they will not do for themselves.

Seen in this light, the brilliant effectiveness of the Social Security System has something almost sinister about it. An administrative mechanism capable of delivering a monthly check to one out of every seven Americans, and of doing much else besides, is big government at its most efficient, yet most overwhelming. The very way the system is set up, with employee contributions automatically held back from paychecks, with employee *and* employer

---

* Ronald Reagan's impassioned espousal of voluntary Social Security during the 1976 campaign ended by mid-1978 when he became a serious contender for the 1980 Republican presidential nomination. During the 1980 campaign, the most Reagan would say about Social Security was that, as president, he would appoint a "special committee" to study it. He seemed not to be aware of the existence of the Social Security Advisory Council, or of the President's Commission on Pension Policy.

contributions automatically flowing into the government's TT&L (Treasury, Tax, and Loan) account at the local bank, leaves very little room—in fact, no room—for private initiative. And the benefits themselves—are they not a subtle way of sapping individual incentive to work and save?

To the widowed grandmother on a Mississippi farm with a clutch of grandchildren to help raise and only her Social Security to do it on, this reasoning would be incomprehensible. But to many other Americans, including many who depend on Social Security, the Goldwater attitude makes troubling sense. As an example, let me refer you once again to my father. As he told me afterward, on the morning of his sixty-fifth birthday the telephone rang in his New York apartment. It was a nice lady from the Social Security field office that served his district. "She actually wished me a happy birthday," reported my father incredulously. "She said my Social Security would start as of that day. If I had any questions or problems, I should be sure to let her know. It was absolutely sensational service." Then he added, in that triumphant don't-say-I-didn't-warn-you tone that from parenthood's primordial beginnings has set children's teeth on edge: "I'll tell you one thing, though. It's going to break the country."

For those who remember the late 1960s, my dad's remark will carry an ironic ring. For, during those years it was not Social Security that threatened to break the country. It was rather the concatenation of bloody events, the mesh that caught up into one horrifying experience the assassinations of Martin Luther King, Jr., and Robert Kennedy, the destruction in Vietnam, and the street violence that peaked at the 1968 Democratic convention in Chicago. The Social Security System was far from standing still. Between 1965 and 1970, retirement benefits went up by more than 20 percent (and were raised another 15 percent on January 1, 1970). Medicare, to the infinite gratification of Lyndon B. Johnson, went into effect in July 1966. Social Security taxes, too, went up. In 1965, the combined employer-employee "contribution," or tax, was 6.75 percent of a $4,800-a-year wage base, or $324. In 1970, it was 7.3 percent of a $7,800 wage base, or $569.40, and people were beginning to be unhappy.* But over the same period,

---

* The figures cover only old-age and survivors-benefit taxes.

total retirement and survivor benefits rose from about $20 billion a year to over $35 billion. This was far more of an increase than the tax increase would have supported. Where did the extra money come from?

The answer lies in the calculations of the chief actuary.

Like the actuary of a private pension plan, the chief actuary of Social Security is responsible for estimates of the future costs of the benefits. These are much harder to supply for a huge, sprawling social insurance scheme than for a relatively compact private plan, and the results are far less precise. But the technique is more or less the same. The chief actuary develops a set of assumptions (actually, more than one set) and uses these to work up his cost projections.

From the beginning of Social Security through 1972, one unchanging actuarial assumption was that for the period covered by a given cost projection, workers' earnings—and hence payroll-tax receipts—would not rise. Given this assumption and the cost figures, Congress would set the wage base and the tax rate at levels high enough to cover the anticipated costs. But in actual fact, earnings never did stay level. They rose. As a result, more taxes were collected than were needed to cover benefit costs. In 1969, for example, the annual report prepared by the chief actuary stated that in 1968 receipts had exceeded expenditures by $2 billion and that retirement and survivor benefits were substantially overfunded. Far from "breaking the country," Social Security (or at least the retirement portion) was running nicely in the black.

In her provocative study *Policymaking for Social Security,* Martha Derthick of the Brookings Institution explains why overfunding was allowed to become official policy.

> The [level-earnings] assumption was arbitrary and unrealistic, of course. Policymakers knew this—they knew that earnings *would* rise—but they found the assumption useful nonetheless. As Commissioner Ball explained [in 1971], it virtually guaranteed the development of [technically unanticipated] financial surpluses that policymakers could use for periodic benefit increases. But that was not the only reason. It also satisfied the actuary's preference for fiscal prudence. When earnings in fact rose, actuarial calculations were revised to show a surplus in the system—but not before.

Later, in a telling phrase, Miss Derthick calls the level-earnings assumption "a conservative assumption with liberalizing consequences."[7]

In 1968, Hubert Humphrey, bedeviled and distracted by Vietnam, did work Social Security into his presidential campaign. The Republicans, he declared, had always been against Social Security, were still against Medicare. Richard Nixon, disturbed in his turn lest he be tagged with a Goldwater label, went out of his way to stress his support of Social Security. Still, when Nixon won, it would have been logical to predict a slowdown in the expansion of benefits. What happened instead was that a Democratic Congress and the liberal Republicans who ended up in Nixon's Department of Health, Education, and Welfare began to outbid each other in proposing benefit increases. The result was, in Martha Derthick's words, "an explosion in social security benefits." Thus, the $2-billion 1968 actuarial surplus helped to fund a 15 percent increase in benefits in January 1970. Another increase, this one of 10 percent, was put into effect in January 1971. The wage base, meanwhile, remained unchanged, and taxes were raised by only 0.8 percent.

These big liberalizations set the stage for the *annus mirabilis* of Social Security, the presidential election year of 1972.

This was the year that Wilbur Mills, head of the House Ways and Means Committee, personally sponsored and rammed through Congress, in defiance of his own reputation as a fiscal conservative, a benefit increase of no less than 20 percent. God only knows what combination of political shrewdness, presidential ambition, alcohol, and the pills he was taking for his bad back inspired the cautious Mills to take this step. Probably, pressure from other Democratic presidential hopefuls had much to do with it: Both George McGovern and Frank Church had endorsed a 20 percent increase before Mills introduced his bill. But whatever his reasons, Mills brought to Congress the assurances of Commissioner Robert M. Ball and his experts—chief actuary Myers had resigned in 1970, to be replaced by Charles L. Trowbridge—that the increase was "actuarially sound." In an election year, the Republicans mounted only token opposition. In June, the 20 percent increase was carried by 82 to 4 in the Senate and 302 to 35 in the House. According to Miss Derthick's account, "the [Nixon] ad-

ministration seriously considered a veto but decided against it."[8]
So, the increase was enacted. But this was only the beginning.

As far back as 1969, Congress and high officials within Social Security (including in particular Commissioner Ball and chief actuary Myers) had considered "indexing" Social Security retirement benefits—that is, linking them to wage or price indexes so they could float upward with inflation. The Republicans were especially enthusiastic about indexing, which would make benefit increases automatic and thus deny the Democrats the opportunity to claim the credit for every increase, a claim that unfailingly enraged the GOP. The Social Security establishment favored indexing because it was the easiest way to protect participants, active and retired, against inflation and to keep Social Security popular. In 1970, an indexing proposal had proved so appealing that the House had passed it over the vehement opposition of Wilbur Mills, an act tantamount to *lèse majesté*. In 1971, the House and the Senate together were almost ready to write indexing into the law.

Along with indexing, another departure from the old ways had caught the fancy of the policymakers. This one was abandonment of the level-earnings assumption. The arguments for a change were long and complicated, but they added up to something very simple. In a fast-moving economy, it was idiotic for the Social Security Administration to be acting like a squirrel, hoarding up reserves and then, whenever the (Democratic) politicians needed a few votes, suddenly "discovering" some of the hidden cash that they knew all along was there. This was capricious. Above all, it was unfair to the American public, which was being made to pay too much for its coverage—or, alternatively, was getting too little Social Security for its money. The time had come to base cost projections on a *dynamic*-earnings assumption, "dynamic" being a euphemism for the idea that earnings would go up.

Support for this switch was easier to gather because in 1970 chief actuary Robert J. Myers had resigned. Myers was identified with the actuarially conservative level-earnings assumption. When he left, in bitterness over the refusal of the Nixon administration to curb the "expansionists"—meaning in particular Robert M. Ball—within Social Security, Myers left the level-earnings assumption without a defender. Shortly after Myers quit, Ball set up a subcommittee of the Social Security Advisory Council to review actuarial procedures. Not surprisingly, this group found that the use of the level-earnings assumption was producing gross over-funding. Despite the recent benefit boosts, reserves were still high. Indeed, unless a change was made, by 1985 the Social Security retirement trust fund would hold a surplus of $282 billion! The sub-committee determined that rather than continue to squirrel away money in this fashion, Social Security should base cost projections on the dynamic-earnings assumption.

Late in the spring of 1972, the Board of Trustees of the Social Security Retirement Trust Fund issued a report (actually put together by the Office of the Actuary) that recommended that if Congress voted to index benefits, the dynamic assumption be adopted. The hint of actuarial approval was all the election-year Congress needed. Toward the end of June, Mills's 20 percent increase *and* indexing provisions were added to a bill to raise the ceiling on the national debt. And although no formal approval of the shift was ever recorded, Social Security chief actuary Charles L. Trowbridge began to use dynamic assumptions in projecting future costs.

But in the course of all of this change, something went very wrong.

To this day, nobody in Washington who was even remotely involved feels comfortable discussing the matter. And this is understandable. For what happened is that somebody—in fact, a group of somebodies—made a grotesque mistake in Social Security arithmetic. The mistake involved the formula, to take effect in 1975,* under which benefits would automatically be indexed. The formula held that the benefits for the *retired* could move upward in response to changes of 3 percent or more in the Consumer Price Index. Following past practice, benefit increases for *active* workers were linked, or "coupled," with those for the retired. That is, CPI increases of 3 percent or more would automatically produce increases in future benefits.

But all the experts either overlooked or ignored the obvious. Active workers were earning higher and higher wages each year.

---

* To bridge the gap between 1972 and 1975, an interim increase was planned—and granted—in June 1974.

Higher wages, by definition, mean higher Social Security benefits. Even without indexing, workers already had a measure of protection against inflation. With indexing, especially with indexing on the same basis as for the retired, this protection was hugely increased. "Under conditions of severe inflation," Martha Derthick comments, "active workers in the long run would get absurdly high benefits."

Severe inflation? In 1969, when indexing was first proposed, the rate of inflation was 6.1 percent. In 1972, when indexing was made law, inflation, thanks to President Nixon's election-year wage and price freeze, had dropped to only 3.3 percent. But in 1975, the year the indexing formula took effect, the inflation rate had risen to an appalling (for those years) 9.1 percent. And as we all know, it was to go much higher. Within five years, counting from 1970, the numbers of those drawing retirement benefits had increased by about 30 percent, from 14.8 million to 19.1 million. But the benefits themselves had more than doubled, from $21.2 billion in 1970 to $45 billion in 1975. After decades of carefully contrived surpluses, Social Security sprang a leak. In 1975, expenditures exceeded income by $1.5 billion. In 1976, the deficit was $3.2 billion. Meanwhile, future benefits for the 80 million active workers were skyrocketing. *Forbes* (July 1, 1976) headlined its article on the issue "Social Insecurity" and explained matters thus:

> Lawmakers [in 1972] thought they were simply keeping constant the purchasing power of the elderly. In fact, they created a complex, double-indexed scheme under which a worker turning 65 in 2011 could receive substantially more in Social Security benefits than he earned during his final working years.

How could this have happened? How could supposedly responsible officials, in Congress, in the Nixon administration, and in Social Security itself, have allowed the system to skid so far out of control?

After the fact, the finger was pointed directly at the Office of the Actuary. In the fall of 1977, the *New York Times* quoted Senate Finance Committee chairman Russell B. Long as saying bitterly that "faulty actuarial estimates in 1972 ... had been disastrous to the actuarial soundness of the Social Security System." Clearly, the actuarial community was highly uneasy about the part played by one of its own. In October 1977, William M. Mercer head actuary Bob Berin published in the *Transactions* of the Society of Actuaries a short, sharp review of a new monograph, "The Unresolved OASDI Decoupling Issue." Berin wrote:

> Evidently, something went wrong in 1972 with severe effect upon the Social Security System, so severe that corrective action had to be taken. It would be fruitful if the authors would discuss the respective roles of the Congress, the Social Security Advisory Council, the Office of the Actuary in these 1972 changes. Particularly of interest are the following decisions:
>
> First, the low cost/high cost estimates, effectively used by the prior actuary and reinstated by the current actuary, were replaced in 1972 by a "best estimate." Actuaries would like to know if the decoupling problem would have been revealed by the low cost/high cost technique. Did the "sensitivity" testing supporting the 1972 Amendments disclose the decoupling problem?

Berin asked similar pointed questions about the economic forecasts used to justify the 1972 changes. He concluded that "neither the public at large nor . . . actuaries should be held accountable for the consequences of this sort of specific action." Out of professional courtesy, and because the readers of the *Transactions* would surely know, Berin nowhere mentioned that one of the authors of the monograph, Charles L. Trowbridge, had in 1972 been the Chief Actuary of Social Security.

Trowbridge himself concedes that the pace and the conflicting demands of Washington public life "drove me up the wall." After two and a half years as chief actuary, he was happy to resign and to get back to snug Des Moines, where his old job with Bankers Life of Iowa awaited him. It's possible that he or members of his staff first put together the faulty coupling formula and then, under deadline pressure, neglected the mathematical and econometric testing that would have revealed its flaws. But to stop there would be unfair to Trowbridge. Others besides him had the chance to catch the error.

Others, in fact, did catch it. Martha Derthick turned up a 1970 Office of Management and Budget memorandum that called attention to the volatility the formula would produce under the wrong mix of economic conditions. But nothing came of the memo. Miss Derthick says in her book: "Political leaders did not perceive the implications of the coupled formula, and the program specialists, who did understand them, took no pains to point them out."[9] "Of course," she adds in conversation, "some people disagree with my conclusions."

One who disagrees is Robert M. Ball, the superbly gifted former Social Security Administrator. Ball was in office in 1972. Even after President Nixon forced him out a year later, he retained a proprietary interest in the system he helped to create. As Ball sees it, there never was any flaw in the formula. "It was exactly the same formula as the *ad hoc* formulas of years past," he told me. "We knew that if inflation really got going, there might be a problem. [Robert J.] Myers said that. But it no longer seemed reasonable to stick to *ad hoc* increases. And if things got out of hand, we felt we could fix it." In a narrow sense, Ball's comments are hard to fault. Nobody, in government or outside, could have predicted in 1972 that in 1974 there would come to pass exactly the fatal combination of events that would thrust Social Security into the red and keep it there: namely, double-digit inflation with prices rising faster than wages and, as the icing on this unpalatable cake, high unemployment.* Perhaps nobody could have foretold this. But still, as I understand him, Robert Ball is saying that in 1972 he and his colleagues felt justified in going before Congress with a formula they knew might not work.

Whether the 1972 formula was a blunder or a piece of policy that miscarried, it was obvious before indexing took effect in 1975 that the rules would have to be changed. But backing an elephant out of a telephone booth is an operation rather more delicate than driving one in. In 1975, 19 million elderly people were to begin receiving benefits indexed to the cost of living. Another 78 million had accepted substantial Social Security tax increases in the expectation that the benefits piling up for them would outpace

---

* When prices rose at all, benefits and their costs went up. When prices rose faster than wages, the "replacement rate," the proportion of wages the benefits would replace, would fluctuate. The person retiring in June might thus get benefits of 40 percent of the wage base, while the person retiring in July might have to settle for 35 percent. This, it was felt, would be seen as highly unfair. The higher unemployment in 1974 meant that payroll-tax receipts were much lower than anticipated.

inflation. Figuring out how to control the cost of all of this without taking away something from somebody was a job no politician was eager to tackle.

Backing out the elephant took five years.

"It *could* have gotten lost in Watergate," Martha Derthick said dubiously, when I asked her why so long a delay. It's true, heaven knows, that during 1973 and 1974 most high-level federal officials were worrying about matters other than Social Security. But Watergate wasn't really the reason for the lag. Part of the reason was the need for time to develop a technical solution to the problem and to rally Social Security's special constituencies—organized labor, "gray power" groups, congressional leaders—in support of this solution. Interestingly enough, two former chief actuaries, Trowbridge and the indestructible Robert J. Myers, reappeared to work together on a revised formula. Although he had been out of office for more than a year, Robert Ball began to circulate among his friends on the Hill to promote the new proposal. But more important in terms of timing, the Social Security professionals and the politicians alike felt they had to move very, very slowly. A remark made years later (in April 1980) by Wilbur J. Cohen captures their thinking perfectly. "In Social Security," said Cohen, one of its original architects, in a *New York Times* panel interview (April 4, 1980), "you have to give people adequate notice. You can't change the rules of the game right in the middle, when people have made basic decisions about their futures. That would undermine people's faith in paying into the system." Did people ever have such simple faith in Social Security? Never mind: The policymakers thought they did, and so they were in no rush to arouse public alarm by changing the 1972 formula.

Everybody agreed on the need to "decouple" the benefit increases for the retired from those for active employees. After decoupling, the Social Security people wanted to index the benefits for active workers to wage increases. This would stabilize replacement rates. Thus, if Social Security replaces about 40 percent of the earnings of the average worker who retires today, wage indexing would do the same for the worker who retires in, say, 2015. For once, however, the Social Security administrators found themselves in an argument. Treasury economists contended that wage indexing would be too expensive. Indexing based on prices would cut costs sharply and would, in fact, eliminate the predicted long-range deficit. But as Robert Ball said to me, "Price indexing would have dropped the replacement rate from 40 or 41 percent down to 25 percent of pay." This would have meant a retrenchment, and to Ball retrenchment is unthinkable, a rape of those millions of people who will be tomorrow's Social Security beneficiaries.

Ball's successor as Social Security Administrator, James B. Cardwell, came from Nixon's Office of Management and Budget. Cardwell was no hot gospeller for Social Security. But because he saw decoupling as the best answer to the financial problem, he did very much want a decoupling proposal to become law. A price-indexing provision rather than one based on the more generous wage indexing might lose decoupling itself the needed congressional support. So, Cardwell felt he had to go along with Ball and the actuaries.

Eventually, and as usual, the Social Security specialists won their argument. After some bureaucratic infighting, President Ford endorsed a decoupling proposal that included the wage indexing of benefits for active employees. Late in 1977—by which time Jimmy Carter had become president—Congress passed the Ford-approved proposal almost without change.

"It remained," says Martha Derthick laconically, "to raise the taxes."[10] This effort, too, provoked an argument. In her book, Miss Derthick describes how the Carter administration tried to boost employer payroll taxes while holding employee taxes level. Another departure from the norm was the Carter attempt to use general revenues for Social Security whenever unemployment reached 6 percent and lagging payroll taxes produced serious shortfalls. Congress considered these recommendations and rejected them in favor of orthodoxy. It raised both the wage base (to $32,100 for 1982) and the payroll tax rate (to 13.4 percent), so that the joint maximum "contribution" in 1982 will be a startling $4,301.40. It was to offset the Social Security tax increase that President Carter announced plans to cut income taxes. Miss Derthick ends her fascinating study on an appropriate note by quoting House Ways and Means Committee chairman Al Ullman: "There are not going to be any more easy votes on Social Security."[11]

The people at the Social Security Administration in Washington don't go out of their way to discuss the politics of Social Security with the casual visitor. Naturally enough, they prefer to stress the positive side. You find yourself hearing about the computer installation in Baltimore where everybody's account records are kept. The Social Security computer center, says press-relations chief James Brown, is the largest nonmilitary computer setup in the world and, no, you can't go in there, what would happen if we let somebody in there with a magnet in his jeans . . . ? Social Security is one of the hugest of all federal agencies. Since 1972, its staff has grown from 56,000 to 88,000. The number of its offices has risen by nearly half, from 926 to 1,333. By 1988, Social Security benefit payments will have gone up from $55 billion in 1972 to over $250 billion. Social Security currently delivers about four times as much money to Americans than does the entire life insurance industry, and does so at a cost of less than two cents per dollar for administration. How can they keep anything this big both humane and efficient? You ask and, by golly, there's an Assistant Commissioner for Assessment whose sole job is "figuring out what we're doing—what we're doing right, what we're doing wrong and to get on to [our] problems" (this last in the words of Stanford G. Ross, who was until November 1979 the Carter administration's Social Security administrator).

It's easy, too, to become fascinated with the random statistics the Social Security press office can provide. At the end of 1978, for example, 58 people were retired and drawing Social Security benefits—in Bulgaria. Eighty-seven residents of the Cape Verde Islands were Social Security pensioners. In Italy, 20,512 people were receiving American Social Security retirement checks. All told, 139,007 people earned Social Security retirement credits in the United States and were getting their checks in foreign countries, even behind the iron curtain. "They did the work," says James Brown, "they receive the benefits. If it's not behind the iron curtain, we mail the checks to their homes. If it is, we work through the consulates."

As I listened to Jim Brown, I thought idly: Wouldn't it be interesting if the CIA were using Social Security benefit transfers to finance some of its overseas operations? After all, Social Security is shipping abroad something like $55 million every *month*. Then, less idly, I told myself not even to think about such things. Somebody in that computer center might be reading my brain.

In any event, the real issues of Social Security are not its efficiency nor its possible helpfulness to other branches of government. If the foregoing discussion has made its mark, you'll know much more than you did about these issues. You'll understand that Social Security, despite its bland institutional image, is much more than a delivery system for money; it's also an aggressively political organization with its own built-in beliefs about what we need by way of financial safeguarding. And a remarkably successful lobbyist for these beliefs. In 1950, Social Security paid 27 percent of all the retirement benefits Americans received. By 1976, Social Security was accounting for 54 percent of our retirement benefits. Much of the gain has come from expansion into employment areas not covered by other types of plans. But much has been won from Congress (not that Congress has objected!) at the expense of private plans.

The people who have built up Social Security are not Barry Goldwater's evil "gnomes, the money manipulators of Washington." They are dedicated men and women who believe sincerely that the past expansion of Social Security coverage has been in the public interest. They have noted that private pensions favor trained, hourly paid employees in powerful unions and, of course, managers and executives. For them, it is a matter of shame that 3 million Americans over sixty-five—14 percent of our retired population—were living in poverty or near-poverty. Even Goldwater agrees with the "gnomes" that Social Security's treatment of the nation's 25 million married female workers is, in his own phrase, "grossly inequitable." (Why this one inequity troubles him when the whole system is so rotten the senator never makes clear.) Social Security does face serious problems. Calling its management names is hardly the way to start solving them.

Perhaps the biggest problem of all is the one that Goldwater and his conservative brethren have spent so much time fanning into flame. Americans have begun to lose confidence in Social Security. In 1979, Johnson & Higgins commissioned from polltaker Louis Harris & Associates a study of American attitudes toward pensions and retirement. The Harris survey notes that "adverse publicity has instilled concern and skepticism among current and retired employees about the financial stability of the Social Security System." The findings must have come as a shock to Wilbur Cohen. Virtually everybody *wants* Social Security, and virtually everybody (86 percent) sees a need for benefits to go up at least as fast as the cost of living. But only 15 percent of those questioned expressed "a great deal of confidence" that Social Security would be able to pay them their retirement benefits. Forty-two percent had "hardly any confidence" that their benefits would be paid. An almost identical percentage, 41 percent, had "hardly any confidence" that future generations of workers would be willing to pick up the tab for the benefits of *this* generation when its members are ready to retire.

To deal with this crisis of confidence, Social Security officials have been pointing out the very real strengths of the system. "Social Security," former Administrator Stan Ross liked to tell audiences, "is far more than a mere retirement program." At meetings and symposia across the country, he stressed such special features of Social Security as survivors' insurance and disability coverage. He made much also of the "portability" of Social Security: "Unlike private plans," Ross would tell people, "Social Security will follow you as you move from company to company, and generally it provides continuity of individual and family protection throughout your lifetime." In other words, whenever Social Security costs bite home—and they do bite—just look at how much you get for your money: more, for sure, than you could ever buy from any private insurance company.

When you yourself sit down to think over the merits and demerits of Social Security, keep the Ross sales pitch in mind. It *is* a sales pitch, but it's not a scam. Even now, with the price of the "product" edging upward toward the $350 monthly maximum (of which you pay half), the package of benefits you acquire is still quite a bargain.

But what about costs? Is it true, as Stan Ross told the House Ways and Means Committee in October 1979, that "the Social Security Amendments of 1977 . . . restored the financial soundness of the Social Security programs"?[12] Or is the reverse true—that Social Security is "bankrupt," and that only lavish helpings of cash from the nation's general revenues will keep it afloat? In fact, neither statement makes much sense. Indeed, to try to deal with Social Security in terms of its "financial soundness" or its possibly being "bankrupt" is to be vague to the point of meaninglessness.

All of the experts, from Martha Derthick to Stan Ross, Robert Ball, Robert Myers, and Wilbur Cohen to the congressional specialists in Social Security, agree that the program faces not one but two cost problems. The first, the short-term problem, is upon us now. Its cause, according to Ross's testimony before the Ways and Means Committee, was a certain amount of overoptimism on the part of the Social Security actuaries during the late 1970s about the immediate economic future. What actually has taken place to date during the 1980s has been

> an increase in projected unemployment . . . a higher rate of infla-
> tion and a drop in estimated real wage growth. As a result the
> amount of earnings subject to the Social Security payroll tax will
> not grow as fast as the trustees projected in relation to the benefit
> payments that those taxes must finance.[13]

Nobody will miss a Social Security retirement check because of these miserable economic conditions. But to make up the difference between tax income and benefit outflow, the Social Security people will have to tap the reserve fund. This fund, which used to be kept at about one year's worth of benefit payments (it has been dropping steadily since 1972) is expected to dip to as low as 10 percent by 1984. If it goes any lower, Social Security will have cash-flow problems.* If all goes according to plan, however, after 1984 higher payroll taxes will gradually overtake benefit outgo and will begin to rebuild the reserve fund. The period of strain will be over.

The second cost problem, the long-term one, has attracted much more attention (I think it's partly because people love to look ahead with a frisson, a shiver of dread, at a catastrophe that will take place—or will not take place—in another century). This problem is based on the well-known fact that if present population

---

* Six months after these figures were presented, Wilbur Cohen was telling the *New York Times* that "there will be a very serious cash flow [problem] in 1981."

trends continue, there will be fewer and fewer active workers in proportion to the number of the retired. Stan Ross sums it up nicely:

> The large number of persons born during the late 1940s, 1950s, and 1960s (when fertility rates were high) will reach retirement age in the years after 2010, while the relatively small number of persons born during the period of current and projected low fertility rates will comprise the labor force.[14]

At present, the ratio of active workers to the retired is about three to one. The tireless Social Security actuaries have worked up alternative fertility-rate projections for the next seventy-five years. According to the middle-of-the-road projection, "fertility will increase from its current level of 1.8 children per woman to the zero population growth rate of 2.1." If this happens, then sometime after 2010, the active-to-retired ratio will decline to two to one. And if this happens, then per-capita Social Security taxes obviously will have to go up.

According to Robert Ball, the increase won't amount to much. "Look," he says cheerfully, "the rate at the peak period [2029–53] is only going to be about 14 percent of payroll. It's already about 10 percent. What's the big deal?" A 40 percent tax increase, that's what. When I asked Ball what would happen if the birth rate dropped instead of increased, he said, "Oh well, we have no reason to think *that's* going to happen." But if the rate did drop to 1.5 children per woman, Social Security taxes would go up to 21.14 percent of payroll. Nearly 11 percent of your income is a lot of money to be giving your Uncle every month in addition to your income tax. But, of course, Bob Ball is right: It may never happen.

By now, you should understand what the Goldwaters and Reagans of this world seem never to understand, that actuaries aren't God and that it's *impossible* to predict what will happen to Social Security costs over the next three-quarters of a century. You'll also realize yet another truth about Social Security: Its benefits and their costs depend not upon actuarial calculations but upon the social and moral climate of America. For the first forty-five years of Social Security, we were intent upon enlarging the program. The national emphasis was upon taking in more and more classes of employment, upon adding new forms of benefits, upon making the benefits grow. Because the ratio of active workers to the retired has been high, we've been able to do these things at fairly low per-capita cost. But now, times have changed. The period of growth is over, and the stress must be on controlling the cost of the program as it stands. Can we do this? Yes—if we can succeed in controlling the pace of the economy at large, because Social Security, like so much else, rests on our wider habits of production and consumption. Hysteria and shouts of "bankruptcy" won't produce such controls. These are simply the silly noises politicians make when they face issues that lack easy answers.

PART TWO

★

Reform

★ 7 ★

ERISA:
Propping Up the System

One bright day in early September 1963, the city of South Bend, Indiana, was in a holiday mood. Local industry, led by South Bend's two biggest manufacturers, Bendix Corporation and the Studebaker Corporation, joined civic groups in a special "Partners in Progress" celebration. The festivities began with a three-hour parade through the heart of town and wound up at the Notre Dame University stadium with speechifying, folk singing, and sky diving as audience entertainment.

Three months later, on December 10, 1963, Studebaker shocked its hometown and jolted the rest of the country by announcing the immediate shutdown of all its U.S. automaking operations. What cars were built, the company said, would be produced at the Studebaker plant in Hamilton, Ontario.

Studebaker's "partnership" with South Bend had started in 1852, when Henry and Clem Studebaker, soon to be joined by their three other brothers, began building sturdy, oak-sided wagons in a red-brick building just north of the little city's business district. Now, a shortage of working capital, the failure to follow

G.M., Ford, and Chrysler into bigger, heavier models, and the lack of public enthusiasm for the Raymond Loewy–designed Avanti had forced a $40-million operating loss. The partnership was dissolved. Sadly, South Bend's leaders surveyed the damage. Seven thousand workers, most of them hourly paid, lost their jobs. A $50 million yearly payroll was wiped off the books. Woodrow A. Rick, president of the UAW local to which most of the workers belonged, called the closing "something terrible" and "a blow to everyone in this area." Studebaker's board chairman, Randolph H. Guthrie, explained that the move had to be made because "we were being bled to death in South Bend." More tactfully, Byers A. Burlingame, the president, said, "As a South Bend resident, it is a sad day for me, too."

In November 1964, as the last employee left the factory, Studebaker formally terminated its pension plan for U. S. hourly paid employees. According to the standards of the day, the company treated its employees with scrupulous fairness. The day the plan was ended, the assets in the pension fund were worth $37,906,093.26. Every penny went to present or former employees. Quite rightly, the retired came first. They were awarded insurance-company annuities that guaranteed them their full pension payments for life. Next, active employees sixty or older received annuities equal to the benefits they had accumulated to date. After these claimants were satisfied, the rest of the money, $2,447,931.08, was parceled out among those employees younger than sixty who had acquired vested rights to some benefits. As Clifford M. MacMillan, a Studebaker vice-president, was later to tell a congressional investigating committee, there were 4,550 employees in this last group. The average check to each of them was only $543.98. But MacMillan was proud that Studebaker had tracked down and paid "all but 13" of these former employees.

In retrospect, it's hard to see what else the Studebaker management could have done. The UAW, moreover, backed management's plan for the sharing of the pension money. But for scores of employees, the result was financial catastrophe. Younger employees could move on to jobs elsewhere. They would soon join other pension plans and begin anew to build up retirement benefits. Time was on their side. But for scores of employees in their late fifties—many of whom, ironically, had felt a fierce loyalty to the company—time had run out. New jobs were tough to find, new pension credits impossible to earn. For these people, the distribution was a bitter reward for decades of service.

Isidore Goodman, now retired, is the former chief of the Pension Trust Division of the Internal Revenue Service and is one of the country's great authorities on the care and feeding of pensions. Years after the event, in 1977, Goodman summed up the Studebaker problem at a meeting of an important trade group, the American Pension Conference:

> [In] the Studebaker case . . . the employees were covered. It wasn't a question of keeping out the lower paid people. They were in the plan. It wasn't a question of vesting. There was vesting. But the money wasn't there. So instead of getting the indicated benefit, they got a small percentage, which raised a lot of questions.

In fact, some 4,000 employees between forty and sixty received only 15 percent of their vested benefits. Nearly 3,000 Studebaker employees under forty received nothing at all. For years, Isidore Goodman's "lot of questions" went unanswered. Some, as we'll see, are unanswered still.

As the 1960s unfolded, more and more cases came to light of employees whose pension benefits, seemingly secure, turned out to be either shaky or nonexistent. In 1972, the Senate Subcommittee on Labor held hearings on pension plan terminations. Every year, as companies go out of business or change hands, hundreds of plans are folded. But during the period 1966–69, the number of terminations had risen sharply. Mergers and acquisitions, the Senate subcommittee found, were causing some of the worst problems. When one company bought or merged with another, it was the rule for one of the pension plans to be dropped.

In 1968 alone, about 4,500 mergers of U.S. corporations were reported. In this maelstrom of amalgamation, no fewer than 26 of the *Fortune* 500 largest corporations were swallowed up. As a result, tens of thousands of employees faced sudden changes in their pension plans. A few were told in detail what these changes would mean. Some, indeed, *improved* their retirement expectations, as companies with liberal pensions absorbed companies with poor ones. But there was no rhyme or reason to what overtook employees. And, of course, employees had neither voice nor choice in the proceedings. The senators found out that when pension plans were dropped because of mergers, the bottom line was "denial or reduction of promised pensions."

In big-company mergers, denials were rare. The dispassionate men who ran big companies knew too well what a complete loss of pension benefits would do to employee morale. What happened instead was usually more subtle—so subtle, indeed, that few if any employees ever perceived the figure being loomed in the carpet.

To understand what did happen, you have to think again about what we discovered in chapter 3—namely, the enormous leeway the government allowed actuaries in making the assumptions that govern plan costs, and the enormous impact even slight differences in assumptions will have on the sums employers actually put into their pension funds. Only actuaries can understand the relationship of one plan's benefits to its funding pattern. And only actuaries can understand how this relationship compares with that of a second plan. Unless you're an actuary yourself, you'll have a hard time figuring out whether you're better off or worse off after your company and its pension plan have merged with some other organization.

As a layman, indeed, you enter a topsy-turvy world. In this peculiar world, a plan that offers a skimpy pension may in fact be a better deal for you than a plan that provides a generous one. How come? Because the employer who is so cautious about the size of the benefit may be extremely conscientious about putting money into the fund. But the employer who promises a big pension may be underfunding his plan—quite legally—on the basis of his actuary's wildly liberal assumptions.

Now, at last, you can untwist some of the kinks that merger activity was putting into pension plans. Typically, the company that achieved the merger would announce immediately that nothing would change. Employees of Company A (the merger sponsor) would continue under the Company A plan. Employees of Company B (the merger victim) would keep the Company B plan. This situation might last anywhere from six months to two years. But sooner or later, it would change. One plan might be, or might seem to be, so much better than the other that employees would be loath to accept transfers to the subsidiary with the weaker plan, thus disrupting personnel policy. Or from the start, the chief financial officer of Company A might have been licking his lips over the generous reserves of the Company B plan. With or without a convenient change in actuarial assumptions, a merger of the two plans might cut Company A's unfunded pension liability in half, to the joy of the stockholders and the securities analysts. Or, sometimes, maintaining two pension plans simply violated the president's sense of order, his desire that the whole company be one big, happy family. And so on.

Whatever the reasons, before too long Company A would call in its pension consultants and order them to do a study. Inevitably, the study would recommend a consolidation of the two plans. Employee past-service—that is, service before the merger—would almost always be credited according to the formulas of the separate plans. That way, nobody would think he was *losing* anything. A different formula would cover service after the merger. This might be the plan A formula. Or it might be a formula more liberal than that of either plan A or plan B. Consultants liked this tactic. A liberalized formula would make the pension change much easier to sell to the employees. But liberalization wasn't always necessary. Pension formulas are complicated. Even when the new formula was *less* liberal than what had gone before, it was simple enough to present it in terms that made it sound highly attractive.

So, the consultants would ready their charts and set up their easels in the company cafeteria and hold meetings with small groups of employees to explain the new dispensation. Only a few employees would ever be sharp enough—or brave enough—to question publicly whether the new dispensation was really any better than the old.

One day, I found myself describing all of this to the wife of a close friend. "Oh, sure," she said in instant recognition. "It's just what they do in the supermarket. First, they make the box bigger. Then, they cut down on what's inside." Exactly.

While the pension actuaries and consultants were earning bigger and bigger fees for their advice to employers on mergers, other people were sniffing out the advantages that might be theirs for championing employees. The 1977 Senate hearings on plan terminations, in fact, came late in the game. As far back as 1962, President John F. Kennedy had called for a "reappraisal" of the laws governing pensions and had set up a cabinet committee to study pension issues. His move had caught the attention of such shrewd Senate liberals as Jacob K. Javits of New York and Harrison A. Williams, Jr., of New Jersey, as well as of Wilbur Mills in the House.

In 1965, the cabinet committee issued a report. As one congressional staff member told me, "It was against sin and definitely in favor of motherhood." In brief, the report said that (a) private pensions are good things, (b) there ought to be more of them, (c) workers shouldn't have to forfeit their benefits if they leave, (d) plans shouldn't go broke, and (e) pension trustees shouldn't make bad investments. The findings excited no one. In the politer terms of a Harrison Williams statement: "Unfortunately, these proposals never achieved a genuine public consensus and little was done." In fact, nothing was done. But a tiny breeze had sprung up on Capitol Hill.

The Studebaker case had made the breeze blow more strongly. On April 26, 1966, Congresswoman Martha W. Griffiths of Michigan opened hearings on pensions before the Subcommittee on Fiscal Policy of the Joint Economic Committee. Famed today as the sponsor of the Equal Rights Amendment, Congresswoman Griffiths was no less formidable in defense of her auto-worker constituents in northwest Detroit.* The Studebaker case brought hardship to auto workers. It also cast a cloud on UAW leadership, local and national. Congresswoman Griffiths wanted the record set absolutely straight.

An eager participant in the hearings was Senator Jacob K. Javits. For several years, Javits's staff had been telling him that pension reform was an ideal issue for a good liberal Republican politician. A year earlier, he had prodded the Senate Government Operations Committee into a pension investigation. As the ranking Republican on the Senate Labor and Public Welfare Committee, he had already persuaded its chairman, Harrison Williams, that pension legislation belonged in the hands of his committee and no other.

---

* For example, her efforts as a member of the House Ways and Means Committee were instrumental in gaining the repeal of the federal excise tax on automobiles.

Javits opened Griffith's hearings with the blanket declaration that "such [pension] law as exists, both State and Federal, is as full of holes as Swiss cheese." The statement swept away the decades of successful pension regulation by the Pension Trust Division of the IRS. But Javits didn't care. Before Griffiths began her examination of the Studebaker witnesses, Javits hit at what he saw as the basic pension problems: "funding, vesting, transferability of pension rights, reinsurance of pension plans, and proper administration of pension trust funds." All of these were interrelated, Javits said, and only a "comprehensive legislative program" covering them all would truly control pension practice. Thus, eight years before ERISA became law, the senator from New York had begun to construct its framework—and to exert his control over its destiny.

Before the very cautious Javits either could or would attempt to exercise this control, he patiently recognized the needs of others at least as powerful as he. To begin with: South Bend is in Indiana, and Indiana Senator Vance Hartke was a Democrat with high ambitions and strong union backers. Hartke had to do something—and had to be seen doing it, especially by the UAW—about the Studebaker case. Did Hartke want to sponsor a bill that would make pension plans insure themselves against too low funding? He did, in 1965—and Jake Javits gave his bill careful attention and due credit. What about Senator John L. McClellan of Arkansas? The McClellan committee, the Senate Committee on Improper Activities in the Labor Field, had dredged up masses of evidence of abuses in the handling of union pension funds. McClellan wanted his name on tough federal laws against the misapplication of pension assets. So did Javits. But McClellan, a member (and later chairman) of the Appropriations Committee, was nobody a liberal senator from New York wanted to offend. Javits withdrew his own bill and publicly praised McClellan's.

A little at a time, Javits drew into his orbit the whole issue of pension reform. It took him several years, but by 1970, he had built up a reservoir of interest and expertise within the Labor and Public Welfare Committee. He had secured support and money from the Senate for conducting an investigation and drafting a reform law. Javits's chief legislative aide, Frank Cummings, had put together a first-rate staff. Now, Cummings and his associates could start the arduous and tricky kitchenwork of putting together and promoting a major legislative package.

The process infuriated many people in the pension business, in particular the consultants and actuaries. Our old acquaintance, actuary Bob Berin, while admitting later that "it did require national rules . . . to reduce or eliminate transgressions," called most of the transgressions mere "foolishness" on the part of pension administrators. Congress should never have intervened. Then, Berin went on indignantly:

> ERISA was passed by holding hearings, across the country, for those who had complaints or problems with the private pension system. The press was invited. This was an effective mechanism for triggering national response and congressional action.[1]

Berin, understandably, overstated his case. But on the way the Javits team went into action, he was not altogether wrong.

What Berin found so shocking, the legislative task-force people perceived as elementary strategy. One who was privy to the operation was Richard Fay. Dick Fay grew up in Maine and went to college and law school there before heading south to Washington. Now an old man in his late thirties, he's with the irreproachable law firm of Reed, Smith, Shaw & McClay. "Business was ill-represented on the Hill until I went into private practice," Fay says with a straight face. But at twenty-nine, Fay was up on the Hill as counsel to the special Senate subcommittee charged with drafting the new pension law. He's coolly realistic about his salad days. Of the Studebaker case itself, which he calls the "trigger issue," he says: "Sure—we knew that the story wasn't as serious as all that, that the loss-of-benefits issue was exaggerated. But the nature of politics is that you make a decision. Is the objective valid enough to let you go ahead and excuse the inaccuracy?" This is how things get *done.* As for the validity of the objective, in Dick Fay's mind there's no doubt at all. "Pensions are a huge issue. The Kennedy-Johnson Commission on Pension Policy is trying to articulate a national policy to this day. We *needed* some law."

The Fay formula for producing legislation on a public-policy issue like retirement is matter-of-factly delivered. "Frank Cummings did develop a road show, with hearings all over the country. That's nothing new." Why the road show? "You need to have [your cause] publicized by the press. More than anything else, that makes it a legitimate *national* issue. So we held the hearings and got the press interested." The big breakthrough, Fay feels, was the CBS television show "Broken Promises," on the Studebaker and other hardship cases. "It really raised the national consciousness" on the need for pension reform.

Actually, the hearings turned out to be more than just a media event. Americans, it seemed, had been waiting to come forward with their pension grievances; at least, thousands of letters poured into the Labor Committee's offices. "Time and again," Senator Harrison Williams said later, "we learned about people who spent an entire working life—twenty, thirty, or even forty years—looking forward to retirement, only to see their pensions disappear."

Finally, after three years, the hearings were over and the drafting in its final stages. The Javits people, reflecting the Senator's almost endless willingness to accommodate the interests (and egos) of his fellow senators and representatives, had consulted the experts on three other congressional committees. Then, just as Javits was about to commit the bill, under Williams's sponsorship and that of fourteen other senators, to its conference committee, lightning struck. The Senate Finance Committee, run with an iron hand by its chairman, Louisiana Democrat Russell B. Long, moved in on the bill. Finance, which meant Long, already had control in the Senate over Social Security legislation. Long wanted to extend his sway over private-pension lawmaking as well. Dick Fay says with a smile, "They'll try to do this: They'll be watching all along to see if what you're doing really is what the electorate wants." How did the Javits-Williams forces counter the takeover bid? "We stripped the bill. We reported out not even a skeleton bill, just a heading: 'An act to provide for pension reform.' That let us do the key thing, keep control of the legislation and not let some other committee come in at the last minute, take over all our work, and get the credit."

Without the text of the bill, Long's staff had nothing to get its teeth into, nothing to bring to debate. Thus, its takeover attempt fell short, and the bill went to its conference committee as a Labor and Public Welfare bill. In late August 1974, it was reported out of committee and went to the floor. The voting results were a triumph for the Javits-Williams team. In the House, the vote for ERISA was 407 to 2. In the Senate, it was 85 to 0. On Labor Day, September 2, President Gerald Ford, talking of the need "to bring

some order and humanity into this welter of different and sometimes inequitable retirement plans," signed the bill into law.

Opponents still sputtered angrily. Paul H. Jackson of the Wyatt
Company, a major actuarial consulting firm, said juicily: "The
new law . . . stands as an important benchmark on the downward
slope into the totalitarian state." Verne J. Arends of the pension
division of Northwestern Mutual Life told the press: "Number me
among those who feel Congress went too far and got too technical." Karen W. Ferguson, a consultant to the public-interest
Campaign for Pension Rights, thought that Congress hadn't gone
far enough. "For most participants," she said, "the odds of losing
the pension 'lottery' will be changed only slightly, if at all." Some
worriers predicted that ERISA would add as much as $10 billion
a year to the administrative costs of pension plans. Others fore-
saw—correctly—that thousands of plans, unwilling or unable to
comply with ERISA requirements, would be folded. Still others
picked apart the undoubted awkwardnesses and flaws in the law.
But the overwhelming feeling among those involved with retirement issues was one of relief that a reform measure was at last on
the books. George W. Cowles of Bankers Trust Company, a key
pension-asset manager, praised the new law. Charles Scanlon, in
charge of pensions at General Motors, called it "constructive."
Most significant, J. Henry Smith of the American Life Insurance
Association strongly stamped his industry's seal of approval on
ERISA. "The life insurance business," he said, "welcomes the en-
actment of . . . this legislative milestone."

What is ERISA? How effective has it been? Is it truly a "legislative milestone"? Or is it something less than that?[2]

The Employee Retirement Income Security Act is as long as
the average first novel—about 75,000 words—and is as loaded
with technical terminology as a computer-repair manual. To dig
into its details is well beyond the scope of this book. But for anyone who's counting on a pension plan, a glance at its essentials is
a *very* good idea. ERISA, then, does these things:*

- Requires pension plans to offer liberal eligibility standards (membership at age twenty-five after only one year
  of service)

---

* Some ERISA requirements have been touched on or discussed in earlier chapters.

- Requires fairly liberal standards of vesting pension rights (100 percent after ten years of service), so that employees who leave their jobs keep some benefits
- Requires employers to disclose the full details of pension plan operations, including investment, in periodic reports to federal authorities; and to supply employees with full information on plan operations
- Requires periodic actuarial valuations of pension plan operations and the use of actuarially determined methods of funding past-service liabilities
- Includes actuaries, consultants, investment managers, and plan administrators as fiduciaries with legally enforceable responsibilities to plan beneficiaries
- Sets up a Pension Benefit Guaranty Corporation to insure plan members against losing their vested benefits if their plans are folded
- Revises the tax laws to encourage the self-employed and others not in pension plans to save for retirement

Obviously, ERISA covers a lot of ground. Less obviously, but clearly enough if you examine the law closely, ERISA was designed not to remodel the private pension system but to shore up and strengthen what was already there. For example: Before ERISA, the Internal Revenue Service alone set the standards of plan design, finance, and administration. From time to time, its servitors issued memos explaining what could and could not be done in such areas as eligibility, formulas, and funding. As we noted in chapter 2, IRS enforcement "muscle" consisted solely of the power to revoke a plan's tax-deductibility. Revocation might well put plan members in limbo—what would happen to their benefits?—but the threat certainly kept plan sponsors in line.

ERISA left this enforcement system undisturbed. Instead of dragging in the Justice Department or setting up some new enforcement agency, it simply amended the tax code so that pension plans failing to meet the new eligibility, vesting, and funding requirements would automatically lose their "qualified" (tax-deductible) status. On new or amended plans, the IRS is still the authority that decides what's acceptable and what isn't.

For the big corporation, ERISA posed few immediate problems. Pension executives grumbled about the elaborate and expensive new disclosure requirements, which *were* expensive until they were put into the computer, whereupon they became routine. Actuaries and asset managers eyed their new fiduciary status a bit nervously. But soon enough, they found out that the government's expectations of them were almost unchanged.* Big companies had been running their pensions professionally for decades. ERISA, which in so many areas merely codified the professional approach, was nothing new.

The major jolt for major companies was what ERISA's Pension Benefit Guaranty Corporation could do to them. Set up in the Department of Labor, PBGC was to collect premiums of so much per employee from each of the 350,000 plans in being. It was to take over plans being terminated, distribute plan assets fairly, and wind up matters. If a plan's assets weren't enough to take care of the retired and of the *vested* benefits of active workers, PBGC could use its insurance funds. But also—and this is what scared many employers—PBGC had the right to slap a lien on an employer for up to 30 percent of the company's net worth, in order to replenish the insurance fund.

For a while, this ERISA provision numbed the pension experts. Before, an employer's legal liability in case of a plan termination was limited to the sum of money in the trust fund. Now, Congress had thrust aside the shield the trust fund had provided and was making pension liabilities the direct responsibility of the employer. This was bad enough, but worse was the question of how in God's name an employer was supposed to report this liability, if that's what it was, on his corporate balance sheet.

Back in chapter 3, we saw that many great American companies have piled up monstrously large unfunded pension liabilities. Were these suddenly going to have to be reported to the stockholders, to *Wall Street,* like bank borrowings and bond debt? Ooooooh! You could hear the collective moan arising from corporate financial offices all over the country.

Finally, the accountants came to the rescue. No, no, no, they clucked soothingly. Pension liabilities aren't *debts.* Unless the company itself goes into a tailspin, they never fall due all at once.

---

* However, the government did attempt to loosen the grip of the actuarial societies on pension work by allowing "enrolled actuaries" to certify ERISA valuations.

So relax, said the Financial Accounting Standards Board in a paper called "Interpretation 3." Only if your plan is *in extremis* do you have to note any pension liability on your balance sheet.

For other reasons—we'll get to them shortly—the Pension Benefit Guaranty Corporation has all along been an ERISA problem child. And PBGC has problem brothers and sisters. One of them is administration. For small companies especially, ERISA reporting really is a costly nuisance. Consultant Douglas Stegner claims that "all employers have been spending a large amount of nonproductive time filling out nonsensical forms and communicating unintelligible things to employees." According to Stegner, board chairman of a firm called Meidinger & Associates, this is why, since ERISA, "more than 50,000 pension plans have been terminated." Actually, many of those plans could never have met ERISA standards. Also, many were terminated in favor of simpler IRAs (Individual Retirement Accounts), which require much less in the way of administration. Still, Stegner has a point. Paperwork problems have dogged both employers and federal agencies from the start.

But much more of a problem is what ERISA doesn't do. Perhaps its most serious weakness is that it exempts from compliance all federal, state, and local government plans. As we've seen, public sector pension plans are so miserably run as to be a national blot. Their exclusion from ERISA is a failure to bring to book more than 6,000 plans covering over 18 million people. In the private sector, too, ERISA was focused on the system as it stood. At its passage, UAW President Leonard Woodcock pointed out that "it does nothing to extend coverage under private plans to the more than 30 million American workers . . . without such coverage." Pension specialist Norman H. Tarver echoed Woodcock from a slightly different standpoint. Tarver criticized ERISA for discouraging the nation's small corporations, over a million strong, from setting up plans to cover their 11.1 million employees. Of course, as Tarver well knew, insurance companies (like his own Manufacturers Life) dominate the market for these small plans. Said Tarver: "I suggest that another round of pension reform should start right away and that it should be aimed at encouraging the extension of . . . coverage."

The push for inclusiveness, for getting everybody into a private pension plan, has been one major push by those who want to reform the reform act. Thus, in 1979, Congress allowed corporations to make tax-deductible contributions to employee IRAs, the idea being to stimulate small businesses to support these simplified versions of pensions. In the pension trade press, reports have begun to surface on such countries as Sweden, Switzerland, and the Netherlands, where governments, no longer willing to raise social-insurance taxes, are making private pensions mandatory. Indeed, in April 1980, the President's Commission on Pension Policy (of which more in the next chapter) began looking at a proposal to "assure a minimum annual retirement income from private employers." This would be financed by mandatory employer contributions of 3 percent of annual payroll. The very idea is bringing palpitations to the hearts of small businessmen.

The day after ERISA became law, the Pension Benefit Guaranty Corporation opened its doors—to chaos. It could borrow up to 100 million dollars' worth of federal funds to get its insurance program going, so money wasn't the immediate problem. Administration was another story. "We were using IRS and Labor Department source lists [mailing lists] for stuff we had to originate," says Len Lenoci of the Operations Department, "and material began pouring in that we had no files on. We had *no* staff. *No* office space. It was pretty bad." Things got a lot worse when the first wave of post-ERISA plan closings swept in on the tiny new agency. By the end of June 1975, 2,255 plan sponsors had notified PBGC of their "intent to terminate" their plans. The projected figure had been 1,230. During fiscal 1976, nearly 9,000 more notices of intent to terminate streamed in. Over the next two years, the influx slackened considerably. But by the end of 1978, a total of 23,756 termination notices had been filed. Of the pension plans in being when ERISA was enacted, nearly one in every four was being ended. Because most of the plans were tiny ones, this sounds worse than it was. But even so, the paperwork involved was staggering.

Now, with its own building and a staff of about five hundred, PBGC has begun to gain on the paper flow. To deal with the flood of termination notices takes 150 case officers. "If there's enough money in the plan to take care of the retirees and the vested actives," Lenoci explains, "we issue a sufficiency statement and it's up to the administrator to close out the plan. Of course, we check later. But some of the time, there isn't enough money, and we have to decide whether we want to take over as trustee." By the beginning of 1979, PBGC had taken over as trustee for 266 terminated plans with over 27,000 participants. On its "watch list" were another 260 termination cases.

This costs money. At the end of 1978, PBGC was running at an operating loss of $39.4 million (down from $75.8 million in 1977), as it attempted to adjust its premium rates to cover its expenses. In 1978, the yearly premium for single-employer plans went up from $1 per covered employee to $2.60, a jump that makes most auto insurance rate increases seem picayune. The increase was expected to stabilize PBGC's finances. But management now sees a trend in the growing numbers of terminations among larger plans, those covering 100 to 500 employees. If this trend continues, PBGC will have to raise its rates still further.

Two even blacker clouds loom on the PBGC horizon. One is the issue of multiemployer plans, the ones that are negotiated at the bargaining table between unions and groups or associations of employer firms. When ERISA was passed, these plans looked financially healthy. While Congress did assess them termination-insurance premiums (of 50¢ per year per covered employee), it postponed requiring PBGC to step in after a termination. The delay, supposedly, would give PBGC a few years in which to build up its reserves. But as it turns out, many of these seemingly sound plans covered employees in such dying industries as hatmaking. By 1983, something like 2 percent of these plans might be forced into termination; another 10 percent, though in no immediate danger of termination, are in financial trouble. The aggregate unfunded liabilities of these various plans are about $3.9 billion. To build up an insurance fund large enough to pay them off as they fell due after termination, PBGC would have to start charging employers around $80 per employee per year. As these words are being written (mid-1980), Congress is gingerly trying to come up with an answer.

The second of these thunderheads is Chrysler Corporation. As if Chrysler's operating miseries weren't bad enough, the company also has a pension overhang of about $1.7 billion, of which $1 billion represents the unfunded liability for vested benefits. If Chrysler goes under and in the process ends its pension plans, it's this last amount that the PBGC would have to cover.* And as in the case of the multiemployer plans, the corporation simply doesn't have enough money. During the early years of a private insurance company, when its own cash reserves are too low to cover any really large loss, the company protects itself by reinsuring the bulk of its big risks. But for PBGC, there is no reinsurance market. If Chrysler folds, the only place the pension money can come from is Capitol Hill.

From this brief look at ERISA and its immediate effects, it should be clear that the drive to "reform" this country's pension system has barely begun. Many specialists, indeed, feel that ERISA has never truly come to grips with the real issues of retirement, or that it does so only in a half-hearted fashion. For these enthusiasts, true reform means not only an overhaul of the existing system, but also a change, as painful as a new birth, in the way people view work and retirement.

---

* The prospect of this $1 billion in pension liabilities had more than a little to do with the eagerness of the Carter Administration to secure private and public loans for Chrysler. Loans would be much cheaper.

★ 8 ★

The New Reformers: Don't Shoot Us, You're Our Children

Jackson Place in Washington, D.C., belongs on every tourist's must-see list. Only a block long, it runs at an angle from I Street to the northwest corner of Lafayette Park, a minute's walk from the White House. A row of magnificent Federal town houses lines the southeast side of Jackson Place. The executive branch of the government has taken over these mellow structures to shelter, among other showcase agencies, the Council on Environmental Quality at number 722 and the White House Historical Association at number 726. At number 736, in a particularly graceful six-story mansion, is the President's Commission on Pension Policy.

Its official handout says that the eleven-person commission is to "study the national retirement, survivor, and disability system" to see how and where the retirement part can be strengthened. Formed in January 1979, with C. Peter McColough, board chairman of Xerox Corporation, at its head, the commission had a $2-million budget and two years in which to finish its task. Like the dozens of other presidential commissions, this one has been churning out working papers, holding hearings, and fighting valiantly for press coverage. Its members know something about pensions. But the real work of research and writing is the responsibility of Thomas C. Woodruff, the executive director, and his staff. The staff has made the commission, along with the House Pension Task Force, a fountainhead of ideas, information, and schemes for pension reform.

"Over one-third of unmarried women over age sixty-five have incomes below the poverty line," Shelley Lapkoff says. Shelley, at the age of twenty-three, is an economist on the commission staff. Her specialty is the status of women in the retirement system. Shelley in no way resembles Paul Samuelson or Robert Heilbroner, the only other economists I've encountered in person. When I met her for the first time, at eight thirty one morning in the commission's offices, she was wearing a white blouse and a wine-colored suit, and she looked like a mature high-school senior. Her manner was soft-spoken. Respectful. Not until I reached for my wallet to pick up the whole tab—it might have been three dollars—for a taxi ride to Capitol Hill did I meet a different Shelley Lapkoff.

"Here," said Shelley, handing me money from her purse.

"Don't be silly," I said witlessly. There was a gelid pause.

"It's *not* silly."

"No." I backed away from the edge of the abyss, silently cursing my insensitivity. "I guess it's not. But let me pay anyway. It's my fault that we're late."

Shelley gave me a small smile. Her feminism is bone deep. But she has ways of dealing with the clumsy chivalry of latent male chauvinists. The smile turned impish. "After all," she said, "you can't help being the prisoner of your generation and your background."

"That's right," I said, conceding game, set, and match to the superior party. Mollified but still watchful, Shelley allowed me to pay.

Later, I trudged after her as she bounced tirelessly up and down the commission's steep staircases and in and out of its offices. She introduced me to Philip Sparks, the public-affairs director, who confessed cheerfully that at first, official Washington had taken Jimmy Carter's commission not too seriously. "Nobody expected us to do very much at all," he said. "In a way, that helps us." Sparks described the commission's *modus operandi,* which was to divide itself into three study groups, each of them focusing on a separate set of issues. Study Group 1 is looking into retirement age policy, benefit adequacy, and inflation. Study Group 2 is examining pension financing, inequities in coverage, disability retirement, and universal Social Security. Study Group 3 is working on the economic effects of pensions and on tax questions.

Early in 1980, Shelley Lapkoff began to put together for Study Group 3 a report on "Working Women, Marriage, and Retirement." The finished effort would be sixty-eight pages long (not counting the introduction) and would contain an awesome array of data. The Lapkoff theme is simple: The U.S. pension system, public and private, is slanted against women, and this has to stop. In the report, Shelley herself phrases matters more politely.

> Retirement programs need to recognize the changing work patterns and family roles of both women and men. Increased labor force participation by women, career interruptions by mothers and fathers, and high divorce rates require that the retirement income systems accommodate a variety of lifestyles.

"Shelley," I said, "women live a lot longer than men, don't they?"

"Of course," she said. "The average is about eight years longer."

"If a man and a woman are making the same pay for the same work—," I began.

"It doesn't happen," Shelley said.

"No, but if it does. . . ."

"Then what?"

"Well," I said, "won't it cost the employer a lot more money to give the woman the same pension benefit as the man? Because she's going to draw the money for eight more years?"

"That's right," said Shelley.

"Is that fair?"

"Why not? Should the woman get a *lower* pension because she lives longer?" Suddenly, my collar felt uncomfortably tight.

"Maybe not," I said, annoyed. But then I recovered my balance. After all, I was an experienced journalist, and this was a mere child of twenty-three. "Look, Shelley, if it's going to cost more to hire a woman, isn't the boss going to look for a man?"

"Probably," Shelley said calmly. "If the EEOC doesn't find out."

"So," I said, "equal pensions actually defeat the purpose of getting women into jobs on the same basis as men." Shelley eyed me with mild curiosity, as a biologist might scrutinize an unfamiliar but not particularly important life-form.

"Jim," she said, "that's not the issue at all."

"Well, what is?"

"You'll have to read my report." Later, I did read the report and struggled with its conclusions. Shelley argues that today, the real problem of pensions for women is not cost, but adequacy and fairness. The median wage of women in full-time work is about 60 percent that of men. Relatively few women workers (the total is about 17 percent) belong to labor unions and thus benefit by union power to bargain for higher wages and benefits. Even though 51 percent of American women now work (*versus* 17 percent in 1940), they're in the work force for much shorter periods than men. This costs them experience, seniority, and tenure, which in turn means poorer pension benefits or none at all. In 1979, private pensions covered 50 percent of working men but only 31 percent of working women. One reason is that ERISA permits employers to bar from their pension plans part-time workers who put in less than 1,000 hours a year on the job. More than 30 percent of all working women fall into this category. Lastly, the years of their lives most women give to "homemaking" earn them no pension credits.

Taken together, these facts point to a real social issue. A good way to confirm its reality is to detach it—momentarily—from the question of gender. Thus, in our country today, one group of workers constitutes 42 percent of the entire labor force. Without the sweat of this group's millions of members, the business of the nation would come to a dead stop. Even so, a mound of evidence indicates that for the people in this group the retirement system is inadequate. Already, more than 2 million of these people are living in retirement on incomes of less than $2,500 a year. Millions more face an old age of economic insecurity and possible poverty. This is unfair. To put an end to the inequity will take some big changes in both private pensions and Social Security. Shelley Lapkoff in her report and the Commission on Pension Policy itself, in a separate paper on "Treatment of Spouses" (April 1980), set forth a series of reforms. Among the most important:

- Require private pension credits and benefits to be treated as community property in divorce settlements
- Make widows' pensions mandatory in all private plans (so that if an employee dies before retiring, his widow would receive an income for life)
- Make pension formulas and service requirements more liberal for those with lower pay, shorter service, and interrupted service (*i.e.,* for women)
- Apply the "earnings-sharing" concept to Social Security
- Remodel Social Security into a "double-decker" benefit system

Some of what Shelley and her fellow reformers want to do to private pensions—making benefits community property, adding widows' pensions—can be done without too much pain. Liberalizing plan provisions to boost the benefits for women would of course also boost the benefits for many men, and would raise costs accordingly. But the most radical changes would be those the commission has in mind for Social Security. A word or two about "earnings sharing" and "double-decker" benefits is certainly in order.

According to the commission's paper, "the philosophy that marriage is a partnership in which the contribution of each spouse is of equal importance and value has led to the idea of [Social Security] earnings sharing." Under earnings sharing, each partner in a marriage would get Social Security benefits based on her (or his) own credited earnings. For each, these would include half of the couple's *combined earnings* during marriage (plus, of course, the full amount each earns while unmarried). Thus, if a husband earns $20,000 in a given year and his wife earns $3,000, under earnings sharing the Social Security account of each would be credited with $11,500 for the year. If the husband earns $20,000 and his wife earns nothing, each is credited with $10,000. The idea is to protect the wife's earnings record through those long years of homemaking when she's able to work only part-time—if at all—so that at retirement her Social Security benefit will be more than a pittance. Also, the benefit will be her own. Another goal of earnings sharing is to free wives from the present legal dependency on their husbands under Social Security.

Earnings sharing favors marriages in which both spouses work. It's a godsend to the housewife who finds herself widowed or divorced after many years of marriage. Husbands, naturally, are the losers. Some would escape unscathed. But the husband who is divorced after years of serving as his family's sole support really takes it on the chin: He could lose up to 30 percent of his Social Security benefit. And because in most families husbands make most of the money (or all of it), they will be paying the bulk of the taxes for the Social Security benefits being credited to their wives.

To see what the commission means by a "double-decker" Social Security benefit, go back in your mind to the Townsendism of the 1930s and after—that is, to the notion of a universal benefit for all of the aged, regardless of their employment histories. "A double-decker system," the commission explains in its paper, "would establish two tiers of Social Security benefits. The first tier would be a minimum flat benefit. . . . The second tier would be directly related to covered earnings." Because such a system would automatically provide a basic benefit to women in the home, the commission sees it as an answer, and possibly a strong answer, to the problem of a pension of her own for every woman. An even stronger answer, moreover, would be the combination of the basic benefit and a second tier of benefits to which earnings sharing is applied.

These are sweeping changes. They would indeed tilt the U.S. pension system away from its bias against women. But are such potent remedies good for the system as a whole?

I'm not sure.

Some forms of inequity between the sexes in the working world clearly do call for—and lend themselves to—legal repair. Equal pay for equal work makes good sense, economic and moral. By extension (and despite the cost difference), so does the principle of equal pensions for men and women holding equivalent jobs and covered by the same plan. But other inequities, though very real, aren't built into the pension system. Rather, they stem from individual choice. For instance, millions of women prefer part-time to full-time work. Because they want time away from the job, they do give up opportunities for advancement, higher pay, and better benefits. But they do so voluntarily. Calling these working women "deprived" seems to me to distort reality. Likewise, today especially, a woman may well have mixed feelings about the decision to leave her job, keep house, and bear and raise children. But by and large, the decision is a deliberate one, not something forced on her.* If such women are losing pension benefits they might otherwise have earned, the loss is of their own choosing. In a real sense, they're swapping the benefits for things they want more. To blame the loss on the pension system rather than on the individual woman is to play down very far indeed the importance of free choice in this society.

More troubling, the kinds of repairs the reformers want, especially the ones they want done on Social Security, strike me as being splendid for some women but not nearly so splendid for everybody else. Earnings sharing turns over Social Security wage credits to women who haven't earned them. A double-decker Social Security System awards retirement benefits to housewives who have never held a job outside the home. One operates subtly, the other overtly, but both of these commission proposals drastically alter Social Security. They change it from a system geared to earnings loss (see chapter 5) into a system based on the idea that everybody has a right to a pension. Remember the comment of Haeworth Robertson, the former Social Security chief actuary, in the opening pages of this book? "Most people . . . after a few years of nourishing . . . wants and hopes begin to believe that . . . they are *entitled* to a leisurely retirement." Where women are concerned, the commission seems to be a charter subscriber to Robertson's Great American Retirement Dream.

In fairness, I should add that Shelley Lapkoff herself amiably but sharply disagrees with what I'm saying. True, she says, earn-

---

* One of the facts to which radical feminists must learn to harden their hearts is that a great many working women long to "escape" into full-time homelife. As I understand it, the "correct" feminist position is that they must not be allowed to do so.

ings sharing and double-decker benefits "are major changes" in Social Security. But they don't make Social Security any less wage related than does the present "spouse's benefit," which pays to the widow (or widower) of a covered worker an income based on the *decedent's* wages. Because a flat pension benefit could so easily become a political plaything, Shelley "has problems" with the double-decker concept. "But if you believe that marriage is a partnership," she said to me in a phone conversation, "then you won't feel that earnings sharing gives wives something for nothing. Right?" As a husband who knows how much work—for no pay—his wife gets through in a day, I felt the force of the argument. As a man who feels that our society, to its own irreparable loss, often does treat women unfairly, I felt it all the more. Who but a churl would not? And yet . . .

"Shelley," I said into the phone, "a partnership is a business proposition. Something people do strictly for money. I guess I just can't see marriage in that light."

"Oh. Well, that's okay," Shelley said, disappointed in me but kind as always. "Don't worry. It will affect my generation, not yours." And we said good-bye.

Like a subway station at rush hour, the whole area of pension reform is crowded with such perplexities. For a second (and final) example of what the reformers are up against, take the question of retirement age. As in the case of pensions for women, the President's Commission on Pension Policy asked its staff to prepare a working paper; Elizabeth L. Meier and Cynthia C. Dittmar produced a fine one. "Varieties of Retirement Ages" paints a clear picture of a confused pattern. Today, *most* Americans are retiring early (before sixty-five). Nearly three-quarters of those retiring voluntarily under Social Security (not under disability coverage) do so before reaching sixty-five. Those in private pension plans are doing the same thing. Mitchell Meyer, in a 1978 Conference Board bulletin, comments: "The dramatic retirement fact of the 1970s has been the trend to early retirement." In October 1979, Kenneth Olthoff of General Motors Corporation testified before the commission that "a majority of employees with 30 or more years of service retire in their fifties. Our average retirement age has been as low as 58." This happens because during the 1960s the UAW won the "thirty-and-out" provision, which gives full pensions to employees of any age after thirty years of service. Added Olthoff: "This is not a pattern we support. It is not only costly but we lose a large number of employees in the prime of their working lives." Unions in the copper, aluminum, and steel industries have also won "thirty-and-out" pensions, and in these industries, too, early retirement is the norm.

In 1978, out of 46,078 male federal employees applying for pensions, only 7,797 were sixty-five or older. The rest, 38,281, or 84 percent, elected to retire earlier. Over 23,000, or 50 percent, chose to retire before reaching sixty. The rush to retire early from federal service is encouraged by the fact that unreduced benefits are available to employees who are as young as fifty-five if they have worked for the government for thirty or more years. Early retirement is also endemic among members of the armed forces and in state and local government service.

Some evidence exists that people have begun to be uneasy about the virtues of early retirement. In 1977, an American Council of Life Insurance survey "indicated that the majority (58%) would retire by age 65. . . . [But] one year later, the proportion planning to retire at or before age 65 was down to 50%." The survey Louis Harris & Associates conducted for Johnson & Higgins in August 1978 reported that "only 47% of all current employees . . . say they intend to stop working on or before normal retirement age," a drop within a year of another 3 percent. "The conventional wisdom," say the Harris pollsters, "holds that there is a well-established trend toward early retirement. . . . The responses obtained from the employees . . . cast great doubt on the long-term accuracy of this conventional wisdom."[1] In their working paper, Meier and Dittmar concede that "several things . . . may cause the current early retirement trend to turn around. One is continued double-digit inflation which could simply intimidate individuals into postponing plans for retirement." However, they stand firm on their findings that "the incidence of retirement at early ages is increasing."[2]

Early retirement on this scale makes social planners frown worriedly. It seems to defy all logic. On the one hand, middle-aged Americans have never been as long lived or as healthy as they are today, and as able to work productively into their sixties and beyond. At 60, the average U.S. male can expect to live another 17 years; the average female, another 22.1 years. On the other hand, inflation has made all retirement difficult economically. Early retirement compounds the problems. It cuts off years of work at peak earnings. Even for those on full pensions, early retirement stretches the time over which income is most vulnerable to inflation. And most private pension plans sharply reduce the benefits for those who retire early. But despite the drawbacks, more and more employees seemingly can't wait to retire.

"If you look at the figures," Bob Berin said to me of his ponderings on the subject, "there's only one reason that makes sense, and it's a terribly sad one. People hate their jobs."

Whether or not this is the reason, the added costs of early retirement are alarmingly high. In a 1978 study, *Retirement Benefit Levels, Costs and Issues,* the benefit-planning firm of Towers, Perrin, Forster and Crosby came up with some cost estimates for private plans:

> Under a reasonable set of assumptions, the present value of each dollar of retirement income beginning at age 60 is about 15% higher than if retirement occurs at age 65; nearly 30% higher if retirement occurs at age 55. The actual cost differences are even greater because of the shorter period over which these amounts must be funded. . . .

On public-sector plans, Meier and Dittmar cited an unpublished 1979 survey done for the American Federation of State, County, and Municipal Employees by analysts Robert W. Kalman and Michael T. Leibig:

> [That] public plans permit workers to retire on unreduced pensions at earlier ages than private plans . . . is the primary factor responsible for driving up the cost of public pensions.

But what most disturbed Meier and Dittmar is the long-term effect of continuing early retirement on the cost of Social Security. By the year 2030, they said, the number of people sixty-two and older per hundred Americans of working age will have grown from the present twenty-seven to fifty. If people are still retiring *en masse* at sixty-two or younger, Social Security retirement taxes will be more than twice what they are today.

On May 2, 1980, the eleven commissioners held a meeting in Boston to discuss the recommendations of the various study groups and to release an interim report on the issues. The retirement-age issue, although it was one of the earliest to be covered, was by no means the most controversial. Lee McDermott of the public-affairs staff said afterward: "We came out in favor of mandatory private pensions. That got the business community mad at us. We came out for universal Social Security. That got the federal employees mad. As long as *everybody's* mad, I guess it's okay."

(To Shelley Lapkoff's delight, the commissioners decided to endorse Social Security earnings sharing, "contingent on further study," and several of her other recommendations.)

When retirement age did come up, the obvious choice for the commissioners was to recommend an increase in the Social Security normal retirement age, from sixty-five to sixty-eight or even seventy, and in the early retirement age from sixty-two to sixty-five. This would greatly ease the cost pressures on the program. And because Social Security is the bellwether of the pension system, changes in private plans and public-sector plans would be sure to follow.

But this choice made the commissioners uneasy. Granted, cost considerations are important. So is the question of whether or not it's fair to make future generations pay for benefits this generation votes to give its children. Still, the commissioners reasoned, there's a "social contract" inherent in Social Security. To raise retirement ages arbitrarily would break faith with the millions of workers who have been expecting to be able to retire at sixty-two or sixty-five. For this reason, the commissioners voted not to recommend an immediate increase. Instead, they'll try to work out "some kind of formula" (the phrase is Lee McDermott's) for relating retirement age to average longevity within each working generation. There, for now, the matter rests.*

It would be wrong to suppose that the President's Commission on Pension Policy is the only Washington group interested in pen-

---

* The commission did go on record as favoring the retention of older workers in the labor force by such means as retraining, part-time employment, flexible work hours, and phased retirement.

sion reform. The people at 736 Jackson Place have a lot of company. On Capitol Hill, Russ Mueller's House Pension Task Force (see page 102) is waging a holy war to promote PERISA, a bill bringing public-sector retirement systems under federal regulation. The Advisory Council on Social Security, which is best described as the lobbying and public-relations arm of the Social Security Administration, is feeding facts, figures, and reform ideas to a growing audience. There is also a National Commission on Social Security and a curious *ad hoc* group directed by Congress but nesting in the Department of Health, Education, and Welfare. The General Accounting Office and the Congressional Budget Office periodically examine federal retirement programs. The Department of Justice cosponsors a study group investigating sex discrimination in pension plans. The Treasury and Labor departments deal daily with the problems of pension regulation. As you'd expect, the staff members of these various committees, commissions, councils, and agencies form a large and lively information network, swollen even larger by the nonofficials—the lawyers, trade-association experts, union people, lobbyists—on its fringes. Everybody knows everybody else, and there's plenty of room in the web for venturesome theorizing and for unorthodox personalities.

For example, take Duke Wilson. Shelley Lapkoff introduced Duke simply as "a friend of mine." Over dinner—at an Armenian restaurant no stranger in Washington could ever have found—he said very little about his work for the Study Group on Universal Social Security. "I just did research," he explained apologetically. Later, it turned out that he'd contributed greatly to Shelley's "Working Women, Marriage, and Retirement" report. But at the moment, Duke was worrying about something else: His job contract was up. Should he look for another government job, or should he "take off for a while" to finish up the book he was writing?

"What book?" I asked.

"Well, uh, for three years I used to ride."

"Ride?"

"Motorcycles. With the Angels, you know?" It sounded ridiculous, but it was perfectly true. This mild-spoken young man had put in a lot of time with the monster bikers of the West Coast,

and he had a manuscript to show for it. Like Hunter Thompson?
"No. Mine's different. More accurate, maybe."

For a moment or two, I sat there amazed. What on earth would
the pension actuaries and consultants and investment specialists,
with their $40,000-a-year jobs and their houses in Hartsdale, *say*
if they knew that national pension policy was being written by a
former Hell's Angel? But I couldn't take the time to cogitate. Another of Shelley's friends had begun to expatiate on pension reform.

Like Duke Wilson, Dennis Snook, who's about thirty-five,
works for the Study Group on Universal Social Security, a body
assembled at congressional behest within the Department of
Health, Education, and Welfare. "We're hot potatoes," said Dennis cheerfully.

"How come?" I asked.

"HEW is federal. Federal employees hate Social Security. For
us to be studying universal coverage is . . . finking, shall we say?"
Dennis wasn't exaggerating. Most federal employees (2.5 million
out of 2.8 million) are outside the Social Security System. They
belong instead to the various federal retirement systems, the largest being the U.S. Civil Service Retirement System. You can easily
see why they rejoice in their separateness. First of all, their pensions are much bigger. Second, their contributions are much lower. Third, under the mango-soft early retirement provisions of the
federal plans, government employees can retire young, take private-sector jobs, and get themselves Social Security benefits in addition to their federal benefits. No wonder unions of federal (and
state and city) employees are raising millions of dollars in lobbying funds to help persuade Congress to leave their retirement systems alone. One group, the National Association of Retired
Federal Employees, has hired a former high-ranking General Accounting Office executive, Smith Blair, to convince his old friends
on the Hill that a merger with Social Security would be disastrous. Under the circumstances, working inside a federal agency
on just such a merger does have its problems.

But Dennis waved these aside as incidental. It was more fun to
talk instead about the *real* issues of retirement, which have to do
with the philosophic differences between work and nonwork.
"For my doctoral dissertation at Claremont," Dennis said, "my

topic was 'indolence.' " I wondered what the diligent Claremont social scientists thought of this choice. "Indolence isn't just laziness," Dennis went on as if he'd read my mind. "It's got a lot to do with the *pace* of activity as well as the *type* of activity people choose and their *attitude* toward it."

The hour was getting late and the Snook explanations were growing more and more elliptical. But the point seemed to be that in a postindustrial world, people were going to have to relax, to stop being so purposive about what they did. In a word, they would have to be—and are becoming—more indolent.

"You mean, everybody should retire?" I asked him.

"Oh, hell, no," Dennis said. "I'd like to see retirement benefits *de*liberalized. We're running out of the resources to subsidize pure idleness. Retirement as it is today is part of the problem. I'm not sure exactly what I do mean. It's confusing to think about these things." There, I couldn't argue. "But . . . maybe people have to slow down when they're young and speed up a little when they're old."

"Sounds to me like a brave new world for the three-toed sloth," I said. Gratifyingly, everyone laughed. Even Dennis grinned. But then he gave me a hard look.

"Serious work is already a privilege," he said cryptically. "Put that in your book. And make people *think* about it."

"I promise," I said.

PART THREE

★

How to Make the System Work for You

★ 9 ★

Retirement Strategy:
Think, Plan, and
Hide Some Money

By now, you may be convinced that your organization's retirement plan is a snare and a delusion. You may have concluded that Social Security is a clever lie the politicians will tell again and again to squeeze votes out of the aging. What you've just been reading may have persuaded you, indeed, that the future is grim, that the American social fabric is unraveling, and that OPEC, inflation, and the lack of moral fiber in the young have made the very idea of retirement a mockery. In this case, read no further. Your best retirement bet is to quit your job now, convert everything you've got into canned goods and gold, buy a small place far back in the hills, and make sure you have enough guns and ammo to fight off the hungry hordes when they attack, as they certainly will.*

---

* If you subscribe to this argument your bible should be the doomsday classic by Howard J. Ruff, *How to Prosper During the Coming Bad Years* (New York: Warner Books, 1980). My wife thinks that beef consommé is better than tomato soup for standing off a prolonged siege.

Are things really *this* bad? Let's hope they're not. True, most of us, whether we're in our twenties or our fifties, just starting a career or just finishing one, do have good cause to be concerned about retirement. Part of the purpose of this book, plainly, is to jolt readers awake from the Great American Retirement Dream. If you've been allowing yourself to feel complacently that the company and Uncle Sam between them will take care of everything, it's time you *did* wake up. But there's no need to panic. Once you are awake and your brain is working, you can begin to think intelligently about retirement and the way the American retirement system applies to you personally. Then, you can begin to gather information and to make plans of your own. Whatever you may believe, it's never too soon for such planning. And unless you're on the very brink of retirement, it's never too late.

To dwell on the *tactics* of retirement is beyond the scope of this book. In the pages ahead, therefore, you'll find few answers to such specific questions as how to choose a place to live, how to invest your savings, or how to make sure you get good medical care. What you will find are suggestions for working out a retirement *strategy*. If you follow this, you'll be gaining the help of the specialists who can deal with the detail of your needs.

Before you can think and plan productively, it seems to me that you must go through a couple of mental preliminaries. The first of these is a negative: *You must rid yourself of that comforting, misleading sense of "entitlement" to a secure retirement.* If you're in a private pension plan, you may have a legal right to some retirement income. As a worker covered by Social Security, you almost certainly will have an enforceable claim to a retirement benefit. But to assume innocently, as so many people do, that what you'll get from these sources will be enough . . . Virginia, honey, believe me, in retirement financing there's no Santa Claus. In the nature of things, there will be a gap between your retirement income and the bigger income you were earning before you retired. Once you retire, your expenses and taxes will probably be lower. But even so, the gap will remain. And nobody is going to do you the kindness of filling it with nice, green money just because you're there.

The second of the preliminaries is the positive corollary of the first: *You must bring to your retirement planning the same brand*

*of energy and aggressiveness that you bring to your business or pro-
fessional career.* Before you pooh-pooh the critical importance of
an aggressive approach, consider the findings of Louis Harris and
Associates on this issue. According to the firm's 1979 poll, "only
29% of current retirees feel they had done enough planning for
their retirement. The remaining 70% feel that their pre-retirement
planning was in some way inadequate." Furthermore, 90 percent
of those who had done "enough" planning felt their incomes were
at least "adequate." But 56 percent of those who had done "far
too little or none" found their retirement incomes "less than adequate." The lesson is clear. As the Harris report puts it: "Pre-retirement planning is perhaps the single most important factor in
assuring a comfortable retirement life free from financial worries." In more down-to-earth language, if you don't make plans,
you'll live to regret it.

Another point is well worth slipping in here. In the past, during
more peaceful economic times, people could wait until they were
in their late fifties or early sixties before thinking seriously about
retirement. Why worry sooner? By then, a man knew what his
work would earn him each year. The kids would be on their own,
the house would be paid for, and (barring serious medical problems) most other major expenses would be taken care of. A few
minutes with a pencil would tell a couple what their savings
would bring in and how much of an income the life insurance cash
values would provide. In due course, the pension and Social Security would begin and that would be that. More often than not,
it would be enough. And with only a few quiet years to look forward to, there was little need to make elaborate plans for the
future.

Some personnel people will still tell you that planning can wait
until five years before you're due to retire. But while I'm no personnel expert, I find five years far too short a period. With inflation and economic uncertainty the norm, and with an average of
twenty years of retirement in store, to put off retirement planning
until you're fifty-five or older is tempting the gods. Indeed, unless
you're wealthy enough not to have to give thought to the future
at all, it seems to me that you'd be wise to *begin* your planning
while you're in your early forties, and possibly even sooner.

This is not to insist that just when your career is nearing its peak, you turn yourself into a worried little old man. Or woman. (For some thoughts on retirement planning for women, see chapter 10.) But it is to suggest that not too long after your fortieth birthday may be the right time to set in motion the long process of thinking and planning—and daydreaming—that will lead to a satisfying, secure retirement.

Perhaps your very first thoughts should be about yourself. Years ago, in a disquisition on how to buy life insurance, I wrote, "You must first of all recognize and then never forget that your own needs are as unique as you are." The thought may be even more true about retirement. What other people do may be wonderful to *them,* but only you can decide what's right for you. So, in your first musings, you may want to ask yourself some rather intimate questions. For instance:

- Do I *really* want to go on working in my present trade or business or profession until I retire?
- Is there some special place I've always wanted to live, some activity or way of life I long to try?
- Do I ever want to retire completely, in the sense of giving up work for leisure?

After five minutes of introspection, you may decide that the whole exercise is premature and silly. That to be thinking about retirement at your age is defeatist. That the best possible retirement plan for you is to outproduce, outsell, and outmanage everyone else in your organization. And you may be right. You may be one of the lucky few who, like the narrator in the Robert Frost poem "Two Tramps in Mud Time" has "made my avocation my vocation": whose work is his greatest happiness. Or, more pragmatically, you may feel that if you can get to be The Boss, then, whatever your problems, you won't have to worry about your pension.

At the other extreme, such self-questioning may produce profound, even startling effects. The literature is full of cases. Some, in mid-life, rush off like Gauguin to pursue Art. Others find happiness as innkeepers in Vermont. One of the most fulfilled people I know is a man who decided in his thirties that being a token black account executive in a New York ad agency was for the birds. ("Slavery, man.") His solution was to get himself trained as an appliance repairman and then to set up shop in one of the fanciest resort communities in the northeast. There, where nobody fixes his own dishwasher, he's in greater demand than the local psychiatrist. His price per hour is outrageous. His ulcer is gone forever.

But if you're like most people, you're neither a workaholic nor a wily dropout. For you, the challenge is to set up a personal retirement scheme within the framework of your present daily life. Given what daily life is for most Americans, this isn't so easy. How do you try to figure out a retirement plan, for God's sake, when they've just doubled your quota and cut your budget in half? How do you put aside money for retirement when the car needs a valve job, your wife is reading winter vacation brochures, and your daughter wants a *horse*? And you don't dare *think* about college . . .

Yet, you can be sure that if you wait to start planning your retirement until the last family molar is capped and the last tuition bill paid, you will have waited too long. Besides, at this stage money isn't the main issue. So, please don't do as so many people do, let the lack of money be your excuse for shoving aside all thought of retirement. Instead, pretend you *do* have the money and focus on other aspects of the problem. To suggest one obvious next move, now might be the time to broach the subject with your wife.

Even if you've been the family breadwinner all along while your wife has stayed home to look after the kids, this may well not be the case forever. The chances are excellent that if your wife isn't already working, sooner or later she will be. If she takes an ordinary job, one she can leave or change easily, her working may not affect your retirement plans at all. But if she's in love with her work—and especially if she's also several years younger than you are—she may be unwilling to leave her job to follow you into retirement. Is she being disloyal? Or are you being unfair? The issue of the wife's career is of growing importance in millions of marriages. Because it could be so important in yours, it deserves sensitive handling. A candid discussion between you and your wife *now* is the best way to avoid a crisis later.

Whether or not your wife's work will shape your plans, her feelings and attitudes certainly will. Even if you pride yourself on being an unregenerate male chauvinist, you owe it to yourself, and to her, to listen to what she has to say about your retirement. You may be in for a surprise! The little house by the sea that seems to you a perfect setting for your retirement may strike your wife as a ghastly, isolated prison—or, conversely, as so ideal that she wants you to retire *early* to begin sharing it with her. You may be worried about money, while your wife is perfectly willing to get along on much less than you're now making. Sometimes, a casual comment is weighted with meaning. Men nearing retirement joke constantly and uneasily about sitting at home with nothing to do. But the wife of a friend shed new light on this male apprehensiveness by saying, "You know, just before Jim retired, I began to have anxiety spells. I kept worrying about how I was going to do the *cleaning* with Jim in the house all day." More than all the studies and surveys, her remark made me see that for both parties in a marriage, retirement means a major readjustment of habits and routines. The "cultural shock" will be much easier to manage if you and your wife begin preparing for it early.

One other reason to take your wife into your confidence is that she's probably going to outlive you. Unless your plans make room for this gloomy likelihood, you could be storing up trouble for her. And your wife may be a better judge than you are of what would be right for *her* in the years after your death. A barge on the Seine (to pick a rather unlikely example) might be an idyllic retirement dwelling for the two of you together. But for an elderly woman by herself? On reflection, you and your wife may decide with a sigh to give up *that* dream and not to cash in your life insurance for the down payment. But wives do sometimes do astonishing things. Yours might joyously disregard the possible ill consequences and elect the Good Life on a barge for as long as the Good Life—and you—lasts. *Vive l'esprit!* But she should be given the choice, not shanghaied aboard.

The days went with Prince Albert when husbands, as a matter of course, kept their wives in total ignorance of family financial affairs. But it's surprising how few wives, although they may keep the checkbook and manage the whole family budget, know anything about their husbands' pensions and other company retirement plans. Or perhaps it's not so surprising. How much do you yourself know about these plans, other than that they exist? With this question, we come to a turning point in our story. Back in chapter 1, we noted that retirement plans are the company's tools for easing its aging employees gently but firmly off the field. But so also are they your tools, and it's important to view them in exactly this light, as tools to help you meet your own personal goals. Once you decide to deal actively with the retirement problem (and to go partners with your wife), your next step should be to master the toolbox.

RETIREMENT PLANNING, CORPORATE POLITICS, AND YOU: A STUDY IN GREEN

In the bad old days before ERISA, employers could be remarkably uncommunicative about their retirement plans. Not all of them were, of course. As far back as the 1950s, a few enlightened managements had grasped that even a very generous pension plan was useless in employee relations if the employees didn't know about it and understand it. The obvious remedy was to publicize and explain the plan. So some bellwethers, notably IBM, GE, and a number of big banks and oil companies, began issuing literature ("Hi, there! I'm Mister Retirement Program!") and holding meetings to sell their plans to their hired help. But others did nothing of the sort. Fear of lawsuits, innate conservatism, and in some cases plain meanness held communication to a minimum. In hundreds of major companies, if you went in to ask for information about the pension you'd be handed a copy of the bare legal text of the plan (often printed in microscopic type) and nothing more. And the lady in Personnel would ostentatiously take down your name.

The 1960s brought an end to the worst of this behavior, as even the most backward employers came to see that silence about the pension plan was self-defeating. In fact, a reversal of attitude took place. Now, instead of wanting their pensions kept quiet, companies began to buttonhole their employees and beg them to listen. Pension consultants and actuarial firms went looking for writers, artists, and even filmmakers to feed the growing appetite for "benefit communications" materials. A mini-industry sprang to life to help benefit administrators produce slick brochures, slide shows, filmstrips, displays, and—most thrilling of all—computerized statements that could be imprinted with each employee's name and current benefit standing.

For big companies, ERISA has merely formalized this energetic communications effort. Smaller companies have had to scramble to supply what the 1974 law made mandatory:

- a description of the plan in "language capable of being understood by the average employee"
- the texts of the plan's legal documents
- periodic statements of the individual employee's pension credits and contributions
- access, limited but guaranteed, to the plan's annual financial statements

All of which means that today you'll be told, or allowed to find out, almost everything you need to know about your company's qualified (tax-deductible) retirement plans. And you can find it out without fuss, time wasting, and raised eyebrows in Personnel. This is important, because as an up-and-coming employee, the *last* thing you want is for your superiors to learn that you're getting interested in retirement.*

Once you've exhumed all of those brochures, notices, and forms from their resting-place in the back of your desk drawer, you can use chapter 1 of this book (page 17ff.) as a checklist of the most important features of your company plan: its eligibility rules, formula, vesting provisions, and types of benefits. With these data, a calculator, and a little patience, you can work out for yourself what your pension would be at various levels of earnings. If you do take the trouble to work this arithmetic, you'll already be well ahead of the pack. The Harris survey quoted earlier reveals that a startling 84 percent of those in private pension plans—and 58

---

* The situation isn't as favorable as it seems. In many companies, the retirement benefits for favored and for higher-ranking employees (and especially for top management) are generously supplemented via nonqualified plans and individual arrangements, formal and informal. To find out about these, you may need a friend in Personnel. But if you're a corporate employee, consider yourself lucky anyway. Public employees may be told *nothing* about their pension plans.

percent of private-plan members over fifty—don't know and can't even guess what their retirement benefits will be.

Your own figures, of course, are no more than educated guess-work. Changes in your job status and earnings and changes in the plan itself could knock these estimates into a cocked hat. Besides, long before you retire you may have switched jobs several times and acquired benefits under plans completely different from the one you're in now. In all of this, age matters. The younger you are, the greater the probability that what you think today won't be what you get at retirement. Never mind: it's still worthwhile to do the calculations. The numbers you jot down will at least give you a starting point. (If you're serious about wanting to plan, you'll update your pencilwork every year.)

As you go over your personal pension file, other questions may come to mind. How well does my plan stack up against those of other companies? How solid are the investments that back up my benefits? Does my company favor the full funding of pension benefits? (On funding, see chapter 3.) Who manages the money? For that matter, which consulting firm is responsible for the design of the plan? A little research will turn up the answers to these questions. Such trade journals as *Forbes* and *Business Week* occasionally print surveys of industry patterns in pensions. The Bankers Trust Company benefit-plan reports are available in college and business-school libraries. *Pensions & Investments* and *Pension World* cover individual company-pension developments. On the financing of your company's plan, the annual report (in particular, the footnotes to the financial statements) will probably be informative. And unless your company is unusually secretive, a phone call to Personnel or Employee Benefits, or to the treasurer's office, will almost certainly get you the name of the company's pension consultant or actuary.

Tracking down more pension data can be useful. (But don't go overboard. You're not trying to qualify as an actuary.) I can think of four situations in which knowing something about your industry's pension pattern and your company's pension-financing policy might come in handy: (1) If the company is in dire peril; (2) if the company is a merger or takeover target; (3) if you're thinking of moving elsewhere; and (4) if you're angling for a better job where you are. In all four cases, something is rocking the boat.

An awareness of the pension implications can help you stay afloat.

In the first two instances, there's nothing much you can do, but at least you'll be alert to some possible problems. If the company folds, the benefits to which you have vested rights will be safe, but you *may* lose your nonvested benefits, and you *will* lose future credits under the plan. A merger or takeover could mean better benefits—it's now illegal to stick you with poorer ones—but it could also mean shakier funding of the plan.

If you're considering a move, you should indeed find out as much as you can about your own plan and those of the companies in which you're interested. Pension benefits are part of your pay. You shouldn't treat them simply as something that goes along with a job. If you can, get hold of the descriptive booklets that outline each company's plans, and draw up a little chart that compares their provisions. If this strikes you as a waste of time, cast your mind back to the pensions for America's corporate royalty noted in chapter 4. If pensions are this important to the Harold Geneens and Frank Carys, they're at least as important to you.

At some point in your campaigning for promotion, the issue of retirement benefits will (or should) become important. It's impossible to generalize about the exact timing. In large companies, compensation policy tends to be standardized until you're well into the upper reaches of management. Before then, you take what they give you. You don't try to argue for a little less salary and a little more pension. Afterward, "rank hath its privileges." As you near the top of the greasy pole, you will begin to qualify for one or more of the special plans most companies maintain for senior executives to beef up the standard pension.

In smaller companies, policy is usually more flexible. There, if you've impressed your bosses, you may well be able to develop your own individual compensation package while you're still relatively young (in your early thirties). This could include, in addition to whatever salary you feel you can ask for and the benefits that go with it, a so-called deferred-compensation agreement: You and the company agree that you're worth a good deal more than your present salary, and that the company will pay you the difference when you're retired, need the money more, and are in a lower tax bracket. Often, the company will finance the deal by means of a life insurance policy on your life, the company itself being the owner and beneficiary. If you die before you retire, the company can use the insurance money either to compensate itself for the loss of your service or to pay your family an income. If you quit, the company cashes in the policy. When you retire, the policy's cash value becomes the fund out of which your deferred compensation is paid.

Using life insurance is a good idea, because both you and the company know in advance where the money's going to come from later on. But there are other ways to set up and finance deferred-compensation agreements. In certain types of firms (typically, incorporated partnerships), the company itself lends you the money to buy stock in the firm. Over the years, the stock grows in value (thanks in part to your hard work). At your retirement, you sell back the stock to the company at a price, preset by formula, that will be far higher than the amount of the original loan. The surplus is paid to you, either in a lump sum or in the form of an income.

Like movie stars and top athletes, the ranking executives of major corporations employ teams of lawyers and accountants, often at company expense, to help them work out their multi-billion-dollar compensation arrangements. These key men—increasing numbers of whom are key women—are about to collect the golden reward for all their years of effort. If you should join these elect ones, you'll quickly find that their problem is exactly the same problem that besets every other hired hand—namely, how to convert salary (on which the taxes can be murderous) into that rare stuff that in Texas they call "keepin' money." The purpose of their complicated combinations of direct and deferred compensation, incentive bonuses, insurance policies, stock-option plans, and retirement benefits in cash and in kind (for example, permanent occupancy of a company-owned apartment, lifetime limousine service) is to solve this problem. "Why not?" asked a lawyer I know, who before his own retirement specialized in putting together these complex deals. "You wouldn't want a man who earns $500,000 a year to die *poor,* would you?" The fact that some companies allow their brass to use the corporate legal and tax specialists for their personal financial planning seems like a double assault on the stockholders. But the same lawyer, with an engaging grin, supplied the rationale. "Look, my boy. Here you have a man who is paid half a million dollars a year to manage the affairs of an enormous enterprise. That's $1,370 *a day.* If this man is worried about his personal financial affairs . . . if he has to take time off to go get himself a lawyer or sit down with an accountant, it could cost the company a *lot* of money. It's cheaper if he can take care of his personal affairs in-house." Lawyers have answers for everything.

Even though you're a long way from being in the half-million-dollar bracket, a lawyer may have some retirement answers for you, too. While you're pulling together information on retirement, you should meet with your own lawyer to go over the details. In fact, at this point the two of you should probably review not only your retirement benefits but your entire financial situation, including your current assets and liabilities, your life insurance, your will, and your future expectations. Why go through all of this now? For one thing, if you died suddenly your lawyer would have an up-to-date record of any pension benefits vested in you and hence due to your estate. For another, your lawyer, who sees and hears a lot about pension plans, may spot some wrinkle in your plan that could be turned to your advantage.

It's possible, of course, that your lawyer is a whiz at real estate or securities law but knows nothing whatever about pensions and doesn't want to know. If so, he or she is obviously the wrong person to consult. Instead, go to your accountant or your insurance man (but be careful! He'll try to sell you life insurance) or to another lawyer. But at the outset of your retirement planning, it's a good idea to listen to professional advice.

From your talks with your advisor, or from your own careful homework, you may come away with the feeling that your company's plan has serious deficiencies. Perhaps the formula, adequate for an era of low inflation, is inadequate today. Perhaps the plan lacks provisions for your pension to be continuable to your spouse after your own death. How do you deal with such a finding? If yours is a big company or one that's set in its ways, there's very little you *can* do. Griping about the pension plan won't endear you to your seniors, even if what's wrong affects them as much as it does you. Unless you have a pipeline into the company's benefit-plan administrators, or to the treasurer or chief financial officer, it's probably wisest to keep quiet and bide your time.

In a smaller company, you can sometimes call attention to a policy problem without being labeled a troublemaker—that is, if you're tactful enough, or important enough yourself to carry weight at the top. Even so, in pension matters, where the problem may be obvious but the solution elusive (and costly), the old Latin tag *fortiter in re, suaviter in modo* ("strongly in what you do, smoothly in how you do it") is a good motto to adopt.

Times may be changing, though, and the need to be open about pensions could alter the way most plans for salaried employees are run. Today, the chief executive, the chief financial officer, and the company's legal counsel are usually the sole trustees of the pension fund for nonunion employees. In effect, they run the plan. This may be efficient, but as we've seen earlier, what's best for the company and its bosses isn't always best for the pension plan. ERISA takes note of the potential conflict of interest and contains provisions meant to hold down trouble. The trustees of pension funds are fiduciaries subject to criminal penalties for abuses of trust. Without special permission, no plan sponsor can invest more than 10 percent of its pension assets in its own common stock.

I myself think employers should go further. I'd like to see companies enlarge their boards of pension trustees to include ordinary employees who are not officers. Obviously, this move would make very little difference to the way plans themselves were operated. Indeed, when I mentioned this notion to Jeff Radov of Howard Winklevoss & Associates—an iconoclast among actuarial firms— Radov was skeptical. "What for?" he asked. "One or two employee trustees won't be able to affect policy one way or the other. It's just a gesture." True enough; but gestures have their value. This one might please corporate employees and reassure them of management's good will.

One last thought about you and your company pension might not be amiss. Since the early 1950s, when the social scientists and the pop-fiction writers opened up in earnest on the American corporation, it has been the fashion to stress the devil's bargain the corporation supposedly offers its minions: security in exchange for the soul. Do you work for a big company? In *The Lonely Crowd* (1949), David Riesman called you "other directed," as if you had no will of your own. A couple of years later, William E. White christened you, after the title of his equally celebrated book, an "organization man." From their day to this, everybody has scrutinized you for evidence of your blandness and conformity. You wear gray flannel suits. You dwell in suburbia. You watch television at least forty hours a week. You play golf. At work, you deal with paper and symbols, not tangible goods. You prefer manipulating others to the direct exercise of authority. Above all, you want to be *safe*. You'd rather have a nice, quiet job that pays you enough than a risky one that yields richer rewards.

Maybe the stereotype is true. Maybe it's true, as a veteran of General Electric was telling me recently (and disgustedly), that "nobody gets fired anymore." Still, I notice that *somebody* is filling those risk-laden jobs and making more money than the people in the safe ones. *Somebody* is staying late at the office for reasons other than hanky-panky with the secretaries. *Somebody,* even in this degenerate age, is trying to drive the dear sales curve right off the top of the chart. In sum, I have a hard time believing that old-fashioned, inner-directed ambition is dead. The arena may be different but the game goes on. The moral is almost too plain. As long as they'll give you more pay in exchange for hard work, and as long as pensions are based on pay, then one way to assure yourself a secure retirement is to heed the Protestant Ethic and work very, very hard.

PRE-RETIREMENT COUNSELING: A MIXED BAG AND A MIXED BLESSING

"Until 1976, the Borg-Warner Chemicals Division at Parkersburg, West Virginia, had no formal program of retirement planning. . . . Employees were called to the personnel department 60 days before their scheduled retirement date, at which time benefit options were described and information on . . . Social Security was made available." Borg-Warner Chemicals has since changed its ways, but according to the Chicago-based *EBPR Research Reports* (December 1979) most other employers still offer their employees little or no pre-retirement counseling. The reason usually given is that they don't want to interfere in the personal lives of their employees. The real reasons are different: the lack of expertise in retirement issues and the high cost of the counseling process.

There are outstanding exceptions. As far back as 1957, the United Auto Workers began a "pre-retirement education" program for its members. Companies like Mobil Oil and the huge printing firm of Reuben H. Donnelley sponsor elaborate programs featuring printed work materials and seminar discussions of retirement problems. And there are strong signs that employer reluctance is vanishing. The need for counseling is growing more and more obvious. Private consultants and some colleges and universities are starting to market pre-retirement programs supposedly "tailored" to the needs of individual employers. Some of these programs are excellent, others mediocre, but they cut down the cost of the counseling and do away with the need for "in-house" counseling staffs.

One of the most expert of these programs is the one being worked out by the National Council on the Aging in company with nine major corporations (*e.g.,* Bristol-Myers, Kimberly-Clark) and four unions. This particular combination of research into employee needs and predesigned counseling materials is the brainchild of Dr. Edmund Fitzpatrick of NCOA. "We've been trying for thirty years to dream up a package," Fitzpatrick says, "and now we think we've got one."

The "package" draws heavily on Fitzpatrick's own experience as a management psychologist overseas. Fitzpatrick specialized in "operant conditioning," or changing people's behavior patterns, but he swears he's not trying to manipulate people into loving retirement. To get people to *think* about retirement, he claims, group activity is important "to break the ice." So also is simulation, or the use of made-up problems to show people how to deal rationally with their own. But when counselees sit down to work out their own answers, the worksheets and other printed matter they use are strictly confidential.

If you're retiring within the next few years, you probably won't have the chance to consult with a trained advisor. Nor will you be able to take part in the type of group activity Edmund Fitzpatrick finds so valuable. But in my opinion, pre-retirement counseling will grow rapidly in importance. (Indeed, I think it will be the hottest money-maker in corporate consulting during the 1980s.) Thus, if you're now in your forties or fifties, the chances are good that by the time you reach "pre-retirement readiness" at

fifty-five your company will funnel you into a counseling program. If you've never given retirement a thought, a company-
sponsored program could be very helpful. But if you *have* thought
about retirement, you may find your company programs too
much of a straitjacket.

DO IT YOURSELF WITH H.R. 10 AND I.R.A.

Today, more than 50 million American workers in commerce
and industry and about 1.5 million state and local government
employees have no retirement coverage other than Social Security. The numbers add up to more than half the total working population. Apologists for the private pension system explain that the
figures are misleading, that many of those not covered are season-
al and part-time workers—the Christmas help—and others whose
need is not as real as that of the full-time corporate employee. It
is never made clear just why a farm worker, a free-lance illustra-
tor, or a town maintenance crewman should need a pension less
than, say, an actuary does. But the fact remains that a lot of people, and quite possibly you among them, must look elsewhere than
to a company plan.

As far back as 1962, the first effort was made to remedy this
lack. Rep. Eugene J. Keogh of New York sponsored and helped
bring into being a law allowing the self-employed, the owners of
unincorporated small businesses, farmers, and professionals to set
up qualified, tax-deductible retirement programs. Nearly 600,000
of these so-called Keogh Plans or H.R. 10 Plans (from the title
of the Keogh Act) are currently in being. Yearly contributions to
them total almost $2 billion.

Keogh plans have proved a particular godsend to the American
professional community. Because it's not in the public interest for
professionals to be able to limit their personal liability for faulty
work, doctors, lawyers, and other professionals are forbidden to
incorporate their practices. Until the Keogh Act brought relief,
these well-paid, highly taxed people found it highly burdensome
to set aside money for retirement. But under a Keogh plan, the
burden is lighter. Although the original limits were much lower,
you can now put into an annuity, a mutual fund, or a bank savings account each year a sum equal to 15 percent of your earned
income or $7,500, whichever is less. You can deduct your contri-

butions from your income for tax purposes. And just as in a corporate pension fund, the investment earnings on your Keogh fund accumulate free of tax. It's not surprising that the professionals, and in particular accountants and lawyers, have jumped aboard this bandwagon.

But because Keogh plans sound complicated and require a certain amount of paperwork, nonprofessionals have been slower to adopt them. To encourage more people to save for retirement, Congress in 1974 tacked onto ERISA a simplified version of the Keogh plan. Employees not covered by plans where they work were permitted to make annual, tax-deductible contributions of up to 15 percent of earned income or $1,500, whichever was less. With the money, they could buy annuities, invest in special federal securities, or open savings accounts. The gains would not be taxed. Four years after creating these IRAs (Individual Retirement Arrangements), Congress liberalized the tax code to allow employers as well as employees to contribute to them. The employer must follow a "definite, written allocation formula," which must not discriminate in favor of higher-paid employees. The full amount of the employer's contributions must be vested in the recipients. If these conditions are met, the employer can contribute up to 15 percent of compensation or $7,500, whichever is less, to each employee's Individual Retirement Account. If the employer puts in less than $1,500, the *employee* can make up the difference in addition to what he's already contributing. In effect, the 1978 liberalizations enable even tiny firms, with a minimum of book-keeping fuss, to set up and fund "defined-contribution" retirement plans.

Perhaps it's because IRAs are so easy to start, perhaps it's because the country is more alert to retirement problems. But whatever the reason, IRAs are proving more popular than Keogh plans did. A 1979 Internal Revenue Service study shows that 1,951,000 people claimed IRA contributions on their 1977 tax returns; the contributions totaled more than $2.4 billion. And this was before employers were allowed to contribute.

Even so, IRA utilization is astonishingly low. Another 1979 study, this one by the President's Commission on Pension Policy, reveals that in the $10,000-to-$50,000-a-year earnings brackets, 24.1 million people are eligible for IRAs. But only 2.1 million have actually opened accounts. (But of the 400,000 eligibles earning *over* $50,000 a year, 52.4 percent, or 210,000, have opened IRAs.)

Surely, it's not necessary to beat you over the head with the message. Assume you're *not* in a pension plan and that you *do* need to set aside money for retirement. Along comes a program that allows you to set aside up to 15 percent of what you earn—which is probably more than you can afford to set aside—and to deduct what you save from your income at tax time. In addition, in this savings program the investment yield is income-tax free during your working lifetime. The only drawback is that if you draw the money out of your Individual Retirement Account *before* you retire, you pay a penalty to recover your money.

Good grief! Why aren't you down at the bank or at your broker's?

SOCIAL SECURITY

In 1950, Social Security paid 27 percent of all retirement, disability, and survivor benefits. By 1976, Social Security's share of the country's retirement and related benefits had doubled. Meanwhile, the share of these benefits covered by private pension plans was declining. Whatever you feel about the rights and wrongs of this expansion, there should be little doubt in your mind about the importance of Social Security in your personal retirement planning. (To see how important Social Security is, consider that if you retired today at sixty-five, having earned the maximum income on which Social Security taxes are payable, your retirement benefit would be a tax-free $4,956 a year for life.)

General information about Social Security benefits is so widely available that there's little point in rehearsing the details here. Your Social Security regional office—the telephone number is listed in the white pages—can supply you with a wealth of descriptive material. One especially useful brochure is called "Estimating Your Social Security Retirement Check." Even if you're a dud at arithmetic, you'll be able to use the eight-step method in this publication to figure out approximately what you'll get when you retire. If you have a question about your own account, you may write to: Social Security Administration, Office of Public Inquiries, 6401 Security Boulevard, Baltimore, Maryland 21235. Forms for the purpose are available at most post offices.

One key point to remember about Social Security is that you don't have to be sixty-five to collect. You can retire on reduced benefits at any time after you reach sixty-two. If you become disabled, you qualify for disability-income benefits at any age. And don't forget about Medicare, which may be worth thousands of dollars to you after your retirement, or about the survivor benefits payable to your spouse and dependent children in case you die prematurely.

It's not a bad idea to pay a visit to your Social Security office well before you reach retirement age. Bureaucratic routines, which can be annoying or disconcerting when they're unfamiliar, are much easier to take when you know what's going on. At the very least, you should make up a checklist of the documents you need to apply for *any* Social Security benefit. These include your Social Security card or other record of your Social Security number, a proof of age (a birth or baptismal certificate or a census record), and your most recent tax-withholding (W-2) form. If you're self-employed, you also need a copy of your federal income tax return for the previous year.*

THE GREAT RETIREMENT-SAVING GAME

If your company pension and your Social Security together won't provide enough income for you to retire on—and they probably won't—then you'll have to make up the difference yourself. While some people can expect windfalls, like gifts or inheritance, to help close the gap, most of us can't. We have to set aside retirement money out of what we now earn. For a number of reasons, good and bad, this isn't so easy.

I've had some very bright people counsel me earnestly not to try to save. My most recent advisor was a woman I met at a party: a woman in her late thirties, well educated, gifted, and married to a highly successful lawyer. Her argument was simple. "Inflation is so awful, by the time you've got the money saved, it won't be worth anything."

When bright people give me advice about money, I grow tongue tied and usually can't think of anything to say to them in return.

---

* If you're applying for other types of Social Security benefits, or on behalf of other beneficiaries, you may need additional documents.

Especially when they themselves clearly have, and will always have, money coming out of their charming ears. But there is an answer. About three hours after my encounter with the lawyer's wife, I thought of exactly the right thing to say. "Inflation is murder," I should have told her, "but for most people, the problem isn't whether their savings will be worth thirty cents or twenty cents on the dollar. It's whether they'll have any savings at all."

Inflation is only our newest and glibbest argument against saving. Older reasons are at least as tempting. Even now, with the sky-high food, shelter, and energy prices we all face, we remain a nation of consumers. Our instinct, fed by a quenchless optimism and massaged by our extraordinary television, advertising, and marketing apparatus, is still to buy. That fact, given the state of the world today, is at once our funniest national joke and our most disturbing national scandal. Places like Marin County, California, and Fairfield County, Connecticut, have achieved world renown as shrines of spending. Drive through these communities—better do it in a late-model car—and every *bush,* fed and pruned and happy, is a monument to what we like to do with our money. The people who live in Marin County and Fairfield County and in scores of other, similar enclaves are many of them well bred, sensitive, and generous. Yet, even as they wince at the ostentation of their neighbors (*"Two* Betamaxes, my God! One in the playroom, the other upstairs"), they're reaching out like automatons for their own next bits of costly merchandise. ("They're having a sale on Cuisinarts, and I want one for the place on the Cape.") What these most affluent Americans do, we all do in our turn. For better or worse, we live in a society that spends $1 billion a year on diet soda, laying out the money for stuff with absolutely no food value *because* it has no food value. We are the nation that has exalted the ultimate fashion-industry absurdity, designer blue jeans at $60 a pair.

Why do we behave this way? I sometimes think of the plight of the great Sir Francis Bacon, during his years as lord chancellor of England. Says Catherine Drinker Bowen in her entertaining Bacon portrait:

> A gentleman, calling on him, was left alone for an hour in the Chancellor's study. In came a member of Bacon's retinue, opened a chest of drawers, took money by the handfuls, stuffed it in his

pockets and went out without a word. He was followed by a second man who repeated the performance. When the Lord Chancellor returned, the astonished visitor told what had occurred. Bacon only shook his head. "Sir," he said, "I cannot help myself."[1]

If that's the shape you're in today, you'll have a tough time getting ready for retirement.

The grand old propensity to spend is a big obstacle to retirement saving, but it's not the only obstacle. Another is the desire to save money for other purposes: a home, college for the children, travel abroad. Even if you *are* setting aside some money, these uses, not retirement, may be uppermost in your mind. But perhaps it's time to rethink your priorities. In terms of retirement planning, buying a home, unless mortgage rates are obscenely high, usually makes sense. As you pay off a home mortgage, you build up your equity in a valuable asset *and* you eliminate a sizable amount of future overhead. But college? With four years of private college costing not less than $25,000, and with government-subsidized student loans available, you might well be better off leaving that college savings account or insurance policy untouched and borrowing instead (or sending the kids to lower-cost state or city colleges). As for travel, which for some of us is a luxury but for others is the fulfillment of a lifelong dream, *you* must decide.

If you do manage to set up a systematic program of saving money for retirement, what should you do with the money? Well ... one Sunday, my wife looked up from the *New York Times* book section and asked, "If the people who write the books about how they made millions of dollars in stocks or real estate really made the millions of dollars, then how come they're writing books?"

"I've often wondered about that myself," I said, and went back to not solving the double-crostic. This is a periphrastic way of saying that I don't know what you should do with the money. If I did know, I would of course never tell. You'd find me living quietly on the Italian Riviera and leaving the *spiaggia* only long enough to fly to Switzerland once in a while for more cash.

Others are less inhibited about giving investment advice. Browse through the how-to books on retirement in your local library and you'll find all the advice you want. Most of it is sensible enough. You do need to know about day-of-deposit-to-day-of-withdrawal savings accounts, corporate and tax-exempt bonds, treasury notes, common and preferred stocks, and annuities. Perhaps you should look at the possible profits to be gleaned in real estate. But what about the following from *The Complete Retirement Planning Book,* by Peter A. Dickinson?

> Runaway inflation hasn't destroyed the U.S.—yet. But when the rate of inflation outstrips the rate of return on many conventional investments, investors turn to the exotic, rare, and beautiful—gold, silver, foreign currency, art, antiques, books, jewelry, wines— which are pleasing to behold and profitable to possess.[2]

True, investors do turn to these exotica, but those who do may lose money. Further along, in his chapter on "How to Hatch Your Nest Egg Now," Mr. Dickinson states that "Swiss francs, West German marks and Canadian dollars are more stable than U.S. currency" and asserts that "investments in these foreign currencies are more profitable than comparable U.S. investments."[3] Don't tell the West Germans. They're too busy buying into the U.S. economy. And inflation has hit Canada at least as hard as it has the United States.

But this is only the beginning. "Stamps Bring Greater Profits," Mr. Dickinson assures us, "Rare Coins Are Better Than Cash." And he makes the claim, which nobody can disprove, that "selective lots [of coins] have appreciated an average of 138 per cent yearly over the past 26 years!"[4] On art as an investment, Mr. Dickinson has this to say:

> If, in 1950, you had bought some old master prints ... by such masters as Dürer, Rembrandt, Goya, Hals, Ruisdael, Toulouse-Lautrec, Matisse, Pissarro, Picasso, Utrillo, *your investment would have multiplied its value 37 times by now.* Other art categories would also show substantial gains: modern up 29 times; old master drawings, 22 times; impressionists, 18 times; English, 10 times; old master paintings, 7 times.[5]

Apart from being vague (which "old master prints" went up in value exactly thirty-seven times? Did any go down?), these assertions are misleading. They suggest that to make enormous profits in art, all you have to do is buy random works by "Dürer, Rembrandt, Goya," et cetera, hold them for a while ("four to five years" is Mr. Dickinson's counsel), and then resell them. But the art market is far more specialized and far more volatile than Mr. Dickinson maintains. Years of study, practice, and experience are no guarantee of financial success. (Every year, scores of seasoned dealers fail.) The art market is also ruthless. Especially in "old master prints," fakes and forgeries abound, most of them undetectable even by scientific test. You may not find out that you've bought a fake until years later, when you try to sell it. And in this market, there's very little protection for you, the buyer, and no recourse.

Yes, you can make a lot of money in rare stamps and coins or in art. You can also make a lot of money by winning the daily double, the exacta, or the quinella at your local racetrack. (Oddly, Mr. Dickinson never suggests putting money into thoroughbred horseflesh.) But you're speculating, not investing. In the gallery or auction house, as at the track, you're asking luck to do the work of judgment. In my opinion, gambling in a game where you're a beginner, or at best an amateur, is not the way to a secure retirement.

Please don't misunderstand. If you love stamps or coins or Tiffany glass or antique doll-furniture, collect it by all means. Collecting will enliven your spirit. Art, too, is fascinating to own. But buy your art for its beauty and meaning, not for its supposed "investment value." The value, if any, will bob up and down like a cork on the sea of fashion. Beauty is different. It lasts forever.

Let's put Mr. Dickinson back on the how-to bookshelf and think in rational terms about saving and investing for retirement. Let me insist once again that I'm no expert. But I assume that when you save for retirement, what you want is a high degree of security and certainty and that yield and profitability, while important, are secondary. Before considering stocks, bonds, and other investments, you might well want to take a look at such unglamorous but useful savings media as U.S. Treasury bills, notes, and bonds, federal agency issues, bank certificates of deposit, and, for an emergency fund, an ordinary savings account.

To me, the various types of federal obligations are especially interesting. When the people who print the money are willing to pay you 7 percent or more a year (on Treasury bills, the rate has gone over 14 percent) for the use of yours, you've found yourself a safe haven indeed for your retirement dollars. Look into the type that best suits your needs and energies. Treasury bills are short-term investments, "warehouses" for cash soon to be needed for other purposes. They mature at ninety-day intervals up to one year. Treasury notes are intermediate-term investments, maturing in two to seven years. Treasury bonds are usually written for periods longer than seven years. You can buy new issues of Treasury obligations without fee from Federal Reserve banks or branches. Your commercial bank or stockbroker will probably charge you $25 to $35 for each transaction. The biggest drawback to individual saving via Treasury obligations is their size. For a bill, you need at least $10,000. Notes and bonds are sold in amounts ranging from $1,000 to $5,000.

Such government agencies as TVA, the Federal Home Loan Bank, and the Federal National Mortgage Association ("Fannie Mae") must also borrow money for their needs. Their securities, marginally less safe than Treasury issues, offer slightly higher yields and a wide choice of maturities. Some agencies issue nothing smaller than $10,000, but others offer notes and bonds in denominations of $1,000 and $5,000. You can buy agency issues from your regular bank or your broker or, for a nominal fee, through the American Stock Exchange in New York City.

For information on savings certificates and passbook accounts, your local savings bank is the place to go. For education in CDs (certificates of deposit), commercial paper, and other money-market instruments, consult any reputable broker. As for stocks and bonds, their number and variety are so immense, and the ways to invest in them so numerous and so heavily publicized, that there's no reason to dwell at length on them here. But if you do plan to invest retirement money in stocks or bonds, you might begin by asking yourself a few obvious questions:

- Can I afford to tie up the money for several years? Can I afford to *lose* the money without going broke?
- Am I expert enough to choose what to buy? Do I have enough time to handle the mechanics? (If not, you may

want to put your money in a mutual fund or a broker's Monthly Investment Plan and pay somebody else to do the actual investing)

- Would some other form of investment (real estate, perhaps, or a private business venture) offer me lower risks and equal or better rewards?

These aside, the only stock market advice I can give you is, Be careful.

If you belong to a company pension or profit-sharing plan, don't overlook the plan itself as a possible savings or investment medium. Many companies now encourage employees to contribute extra money to such plans. Some offer special "savings plans" or "thrift plans." These entitle employees to contribute up to 10 percent of their salaries, through payroll deductions, to company-sponsored investment programs. The individual may even be able to choose from among several different investment funds, each one with its own "mix" of investments. Often, the company will subsidize employee savings by adding a dollar of its own to every two, three, or four the employee contributes. Plans like these are excellent ways to save for retirement. At no cost to you, your money is professionally managed by fiduciaries. You pay no federal income tax on the gains. (There's a move afoot to make your contributions, too, tax deductible.) Your company may be supplementing your savings. When you retire, the money is waiting for you.

One final and very obvious point about investing for retirement is that the younger you are when you start, the better. Not only do you give yourself more time in which to accumulate the money you need, but you also buy yourself a margin of time to make up losses and remedy defects in your program. Unless yours is a special situation, you should diversify your investments to spread the risk of loss. But time and consistency, not necessarily the type of investment you make, are your best guarantors of success.

★ **10** ★

Women and Retirement: How Not to Be the Poorer Sex

Women today live a lot longer than men and earn a lot less, or earn no money at all. For millions of women, these facts add up to serious retirement problems. Women who hold jobs often fail to qualify for employer-sponsored pensions (see chapter 7). Even if they do qualify, their actual benefits may be tiny because they're not at work long enough to build up substantial service and earnings credits. Married women who stay at home face other types of problems. As economic dependents, they will follow their husbands into retirement. Obviously, the adequacy of their husbands' pension and Social Security benefits is of keen concern to them. And what if a husband dies before retirement? Does his widow still receive his pension?

All of this seems to me reason enough to devote this chapter to some of the retirement issues that confront women. And the statistics of longevity provide a powerful supporting argument. It's a commonplace that women can expect to outlive men. But you may be surprised to learn by how much—and surprised, too, to discover that the longer you live, the longer you can expect to live. The figures speak for themselves:

YOUR EXPECTATION OF LIFE

Your Age Now	*The Age to Which You Should Live*	
	FEMALE	MALE
25	78.8	71.8
30	79.0	72.2
35	79.2	72.6
40	79.5	73.1
45	79.9	73.7
50	80.4	74.5
55	81.2	75.6
60	82.1	77.0
65	83.3	78.9
70	84.7	81.1
75	86.0	83.7
80	89.0	86.9

To sum up the obvious, you can expect to outlive by at least twenty years your normal working lifetime. And in all likelihood, you will outlive the man you marry. These would seem to me ample reasons for women to think hard about retirement.

WORKING WOMEN
AND RETIREMENT PLANNING

You may be in your late teens or early twenties, just out of school and starting your first full-time job, with retirement a lifetime away. You may be married and the mother of children, and at work because your family needs the second income (and you need to get out of the house). Or you could be in your thirties, forties, or older, single or married, but settled securely in a business or a professional career. In each case, and of course there are scores of others, your interest in your own retirement and the type of planning you do now will be vastly different.

Whatever your situation, the one thing you should do is gather as much information as you can about the pension and other retirement plans your employer offers. Today, if you work full time, you can join most corporate plans as soon as you reach twenty-five and complete one full year of service. Even though you may be years away from actually "owning" your benefits, pension credits will begin to build up for you, and you should know how much these are each year. Such information should be easy to obtain. If you work for a business, you must be given literature describing your benefits. If it's a sizable company, you'll probably also receive a yearly statement showing you exactly what pension benefits have accrued to you to date. If your employer doesn't supply the information, check with Personnel. Check also to see if your employer's plan is contributory, or if there's a company savings or thrift plan. As noted in the previous chapter, such plans are excellent savings media. (By the way, if you leave your job, your employer must pay over to you any contributions you've made to such cash-benefit plans, plus interest.)

Part of the reason for this book is to demystify pension plans, but no book can cover all the details. If any of the fine points of your employer's plan puzzle or trouble you, don't hesitate to ask questions and to press for comprehensible answers. One of the hardest but most important lessons working women must learn is a lesson in polite persistence. You need accurate information. Don't be too embarrassed or too shy to ask for it.

If there is no retirement plan where you work, you should seriously consider setting up your own IRA (Individual Retirement Account). Even if you're a very young woman—perhaps I should say *especially* if you're a very young woman—the idea of setting aside money of your own for your own future should have strong appeal. The tax advantages of IRAs have already been described (pages 186–88). The financial advantages speak for themselves. (To give you an idea of what they are, if you can put $50 a month into an IRA at 8 percent interest, and you do so from the time you're twenty-five to the day you reach sixty-five, you'll have accumulated more than $75,000.) Above all, the emotional advantages of having a fund of your own, independent of a husband or anyone else, could be enormous.

We've also seen in earlier chapters that far-reaching changes are in prospect for Social Security. Even if you are in a pension plan, remember that Social Security today pays close to 60 percent of all retirement benefits. You could change jobs and lose your present pension benefits. You could drop out of the work force for years—or forever. Your husband might then make you financially secure. But he might not, and it's quite possible that most or all of *your* retirement income will come from the Social Security "spouse benefit," which is based on *his* earnings. In other words, at present, your position as a married homemaker is one of dependency. This is another strong reason why you should start an IRA, or at least a savings account, that is entirely your own. In any case, do familiarize yourself with Social Security, and, if only through the newspapers, keep abreast of changes in the program.

"ARRANGEMENTS"

If you decide to live with a lover, the practical arrangements often take on a charm of their own. If you're both working, you may simply decide to go halves on the household expenses (food, rent, phone, utilities, insurance) and that each of you will retain her (or his) share of the "capital" of the relationship: the furniture, the car, the stereo. So far, so okay. But if either party has additional capital, be it savings accounts, stocks and bonds, real estate, or whatever, be careful! You may need a written memorandum or other formal ownership agreement. It may even pay you to retain a lawyer to draw one up.

For young couples, retirement benefits scarcely ever figure in these arrangements. But if you're in your thirties or older and are planning to share your life with someone else, you should at least be aware of the issue. You yourself may belong to a good pension plan. You may in fact have substantial vested benefits. Does your partner? If he begged you hard enough, are there contributions you could withdraw to turn over to him? It may sound mean-spirited, but while you might gladly share most of your money with your lover, your retirement money should in my opinion be kept beyond *anyone* else's reach.

The classic difficulty, of course, comes from an arrangement between a younger woman and an older man. Often, a woman will enter into such a relationship in the belief that her partner will look after her financially as well as emotionally. For a while, perhaps for many years, he does so. Then, abruptly, the man deserts, or suddenly dies. Only then does the woman realize that her lover has made no provision at all for her support. And by then, she may be too old to find a decent job, or indeed any job, let alone be able to set aside money for retirement.

In the old days, when a man kept a mistress his gentleman's code obliged him to support her. There would be a small apartment—and he would pay the rent. There would be a household allowance. There might or might not be footmen and jewels and a villa at Antibes. But an annuity there would certainly be, for the time when beauty faded and charm fled.

You may loathe—or laugh at—the idea of being a kept woman. But if your companion is an older man, this places on *you* the responsibility for looking after yourself in retirement. It may be unromantic, even mercenary. But perhaps your wisest move is to discuss the situation with your lover. Then, whatever happens, you'll know exactly where you stand.

MARRIAGE

Whatever marriage means in American society today, it no longer means the total economic dependency of wife upon husband. In millions of marriages, it's true, the roles of breadwinner and homemaker are played as tradition dictates. But in millions more, wives too are winning a share of the bread, and are winning for themselves and for other married women a larger voice in the financial decision making. In chapter 8, I urged husbands to give ear to their wives' ideas and wishes in planning retirement. Now let me urge wives to accept the challenge and come forward. Many of you, indeed, will have to take the first step. A husband may be as brave as a lion about reseeding the lawn, facing surgery, or deciding where the children should go to college. But when it comes to retirement, he may be a scared little boy, too frightened even to think about the awful day when he'll have to bid his job farewell. If asked, he may simply grunt, "I've got a plan at the office that takes care of that" or some other phrase that really means "Go away and don't bother me."

You don't need to be a psychiatrist to figure out why he's sticking his head deep into the sand. It's par for the course. For many men, and for successful men especially, the job is the mainstay of the ego. What others think of your husband largely depends on what he does for a living and how well—as measured by your style of life—he does it. More important, these same matters govern what your husband thinks of himself. Raise the question of retirement and, along with perfectly legitimate worries about health, finances, and so on, you raise the spectre of his forthcoming personal diminishment and slippage of identity.

How you overcome husbandly reluctance to consider retirement depends on your knowledge and understanding of the man you married. Maybe your husband will respond to gentle questioning. Maybe you'll have to needle him. Be persistent! If all else fails, you might try a direct frontal attack. Show your husband the life-expectancy figures on page 197. Then tell him bluntly that he has no right to keep you in the dark about an old age he might not be around to share with you.

If you can persuade your husband that retirement is something to be planned jointly, the two of you might make a list of the chores your planning will require. Among these is a close look at his company's retirement literature. Most of what you'll be looking for has already been covered in chapter 8. But as a wife, you should also check to see whether or not your husband's plan includes a so-called widow's benefit. This is a provision under which you would receive an income for life if your husband died *before* retiring. Some plans do offer such a benefit, others do not. If your husband's does not, the lack is not necessarily a black mark against the plan. Many benefit-plan designers feel that a widow's benefit should be financed through group life insurance rather than through the pension plan. If your husband's group life insurance certificate shows that he's covered for more than the usual two to three times annual salary, the chances are that his company has chosen insurance as the medium for a widow's benefit.

Another thing to look for in his pension plan is a disability benefit. For obvious reasons, the lengthy disability of the breadwinner is one of the worst disasters that can overtake a family. Originally, as noted in chapter 2, pension plans primarily covered disabilities and seldom provided old-age benefits. Now the reverse is true. But some private plans and almost all public-employee plans still are the vehicles for income payments to disabled employees. Again, if you find no disability provision in your husband's plan, don't give up your search. Like widow's benefits, disability benefits are often insured today instead of being made part of the pension.

If your husband has no company pension plan, he may have established either a Keogh plan (see pages 186–87) or an IRA. If not, and if the family finances can afford *any* savings, an IRA is an obvious next step. If you're both working, by the way, and neither of you has company pension coverage, you can each put money into an IRA, up to a combined maximum of 15 percent of your income or, if less, $3,000 a year.

Now, let's shift our focus. You are fifty and, you assume, happily married to a man your own age. One day, you're tidying up his den and you come across a letter in unfamiliar handwriting. God forgive you, you read it. And your world turns upside down. Remember that cute blonde ski instructress who was giving your husband his lessons at Sugarbush last winter? Well, she's still giving him lessons, and here it is July.

When you get over the shock, you decide you want only one thing from your husband—a divorce. Yet you're fifty. You've aged well (everybody says so), you've kept your figure, you're not so bad on skis yourself. Still . . . you're fifty. On your way to being old. Suddenly, you realize that there's not enough time for you to break away and start all over again.

Soap opera stuff? Certainly. But it happens in real life to thousands of women a year. Love and respect have drained out of their marriages. All that remains is economic need. Because of it, they have no choice but to stay married and to accept whatever humiliation or neglect their husbands inflict upon them. Could anything like this happen to you? Heaven forbid. But let me remind you that money of your own can be the key to avoiding an imprisoning marriage. It seems to me that every married woman should find a way to put by *some* money that's hers alone. Maybe it's a few thousand dollars scraped together out of the household budget over the years. Maybe it's that little legacy Aunt Augusta left you, which you were going to use for a mink jacket or a trip to Mexico. Maybe it's money your husband himself gives you to spend or to save as you please. But whatever the source, set it aside until you know you'll never need it, not ever.

DIVORCE

"Today," reports the President's Commission on Pension Policy, "the probability is about one in three that a new marriage will end in divorce." And the statistics for established marriages are hardly more cheery. In a word, whatever your age and your income bracket, divorce can happen to you. And perhaps it should.

If you and your husband are both young, his retirement benefits (or yours) will probably count for little or nothing in the bargaining over a divorce settlement. But if you're in your late thirties or older, and if your husband has worked for the same employer for ten years or more, his vested pension benefits may already be worth a good deal of money. Also, his own contributions to a pension or profit-sharing plan may add up to a respectable sum. In community-property states,* the courts will recognize your right to a half-share in some part of your husband's retirement benefits. But just which portion is considered community property is at present a wide-open question. Thus, in California a couple of recent malpractice lawsuits against divorce lawyers have jolted the legal community awake on the pension issue. In both cases, the lawyers neglected to include pension benefits in their settlement reckonings, were sued by their unhappy clients—and lost. As a result, California divorce lawyers are going after not only vested pension-benefits but also the value of pension-income payments, even if these won't begin for years and might not *ever* be due. In Texas, however, they do things differently. Texas is a community-property state. But there, I'm told, the judges don't call pension benefits property, let alone community property, until the benefits are actually being paid.

In the thirty-five non-community-property states, deciding what property is subject to divorce claims is left to the lawyers for the parties. Often, the problem is simply that your lawyer, his eye on such tangible assets as the house, the car, the weekend place, the bank accounts, the stocks, and the life insurance policies, for-

---

* Arizona, California, Idaho, Louisiana, Nevada, New Mexico, Texas, and Washington. In addition, six states accept the principle of community property in divorce settlements only.

gets all about the retirement plans. You may have to issue him a reminder!

A problem of a different sort may arise if your husband is already retired and if the court awards you a share of his income benefits. If *he* has to write you a check each month, you may never see any money. You're probably better off getting your money directly from the employer. But employers are often unhappy about paying pension benefits to anyone except the pensioner. A call from your lawyer may thus be necessary to smooth out the difficulty.

Epilogue

If you began this book as a dreamer of "the Great American Retirement Dream," by now you should certainly be wide awake.

You've wandered briefly through the Marienbad maze of the dream itself, as created by the merchants who peddle their wares to the aging.

You've seen how our industrial society—brilliantly—has turned the very idea of a secure retirement into the subtlest of rewards for long, productive service. And into the least cruel of punishments for the one crime of which everybody in America will eventually be guilty, the crime of growing old.

A glance back into history has shown you the understory, in mathematics and philosophy and social action, of what has become today's enormous retirement industry. More pragmatically, you've seen how this industry operates. You've had a look at how actuaries design and sell retirement plans and keep track of their costs, and at how investment specialists deal with all the money and with each other.

From your survey of public-sector plans, you can rest assured that we've by no means turned into a nation of do-gooders. Favoritism and caprice, incompetence and dishonesty, double-dealing and greed are still alive and well in statehouses, city halls, and county seats across the country.

In your review of Social Security, you've seen how gifted, dedicated people have tried to deal with problems of old age and poverty not solvable by private effort on any scale. And you've seen how, in the process, those public servants have come dangerously close to building a system that cannot survive its own success.

As you've followed the efforts of the reformers, you've gained insight into the unfairness that time and tradition have built into our public and private retirement systems. You now know how many millions of people lack adequate old-age coverage and how unevenly the system showers money on those who do qualify. Reform, I hope you'll agree, is long overdue.

Finally, you've had driven home the basic message of this book. As important as are the big retirement systems to which most of us belong, they by themselves can almost never solve our personal financial needs at retirement. At best, they are a base on which to build. To secure a comfortable retirement, each of us must also put into play some rather old-fashioned virtues: initiative, perseverance, thrift, self-denial. These *are* old-fashioned virtues. But their names ring sweetly to the ear.

Notes

INTRODUCTION

1. A. Haeworth Robertson, *Social Security: Prospect For Change.* New York: Brochure privately printed for William M. Mercer, Inc., 1978, pp. 23–24.
2. *Ibid.,* p. 20.
3. A. F. Ehrbar, "Those Pension Funds Are Even Weaker Than You Think." *Fortune,* November 1977, pp. 104–5.

CHAPTER 1

1. Fortune Market Research, *How Major Industrial Corporations View Employee Benefit Programs.* New York: Fortune, 1974, p. 5.
2. *Employer Attitudes Toward Mandatory Retirement.* New York: Survey report privately printed for William M. Mercer, Inc., June 1977, p. 7.

CHAPTER 2

1. Saul K. Padover, ed., *The Washington Papers: Basic Selections From the Public and Private Writings of George Washington.* New York: Grosset & Dunlap Universal Library, 1967, pp. 81, 94.
2. Richard Hofstadter, *The American Political Tradition and the Men Who Made It.* New York: Vintage Books, 1954, p. 57.
3. Lawrence A. Cremin, *Traditions of American Education.* New York: Basic Books, 1977, pp. 71–72.
4. Daniel J. Boorstin, *The Americans: The National Experience.* New York: Vintage Books, 1967, p. 29.
5. Alfred D. Chandler, Jr., *The Visible Hand.* Cambridge, Massachusetts: The Harvard University Press, 1979, p. 92.
6. *Ibid.,* p. 94.
7. *Ibid.,* p. 95.
8. *Ibid.*
9. Murray Webb Latimer, *Industrial Pension Systems.* New York: Industrial Relations Counselors, Inc., 1933, p. 18.
10. F. A. Vanderlip, speech before the Conference of Charities and Corrections, Philadelphia, Pennsylvania, 1906. In Lee Welling Squier, *Old Age Dependency in the United States.* New York: The Macmillan Company, 1912, p. 73.
11. *Loc. cit.*
12. Joseph Frazier Wall, *Andrew Carnegie.* New York: Oxford University Press, 1970, p. 872.
13. Peter Collier and David Horowitz, *The Rockefellers.* New York: Holt, Rinehart and Winston, 1976, p. 142.
14. Latimer, *op. cit.,* p. 18.
15. *Industrial Pensions in the United States.* New York: The National Industrial Conference Board, 1925, p. 6.
16. Emil Ludwig, *Bismarck, The Story of A Fighter.* Boston: Little, Brown and Company, 1927, pp. 548–49.
17. *Pensions—Intricate and Expensive.* New York: Brochure privately printed for Johnson & Higgins, n.d., p. 3.

CHAPTER 3

1. John Brooks, *Conflicts of Interest: Corporate Pension Fund Asset Management.* New York: The Twentieth Century Fund, 1975, p. 34.

CHAPTER 4

1. Martin Mayer, *The Bankers.* New York: Ballantine Books, 1976, pp. 515ff.
2. Adam Smith [*pseud.* George J. G. Goodman], *Supermoney.* New York: Popular Library, 1972, p. 176.
3. John Brooks, *The Go-Go Years.* New York: Weybright and Talley, 1973, p. 184.
4. Adam Smith, *op. cit.,* p. 88.

CHAPTER 5

1. Steven Brill, *The Teamsters.* New York: Pocket Books, 1979, p. 254.
2. Damodar Gujarati, *Pension Funds and New York City's Fiscal Crisis.* Washington, D.C.: American Enterprise Institute for Public Policy Research, 1978, p. 55.
3. Theodore H. White, *The Making of the President, 1972.* New York: Atheneum Publishers, 1973, pp. 151–52.
4. Howard E. Winklevoss and Dan M. McGill, *Public Pension Plans.* Homewood, Illinois: Dow Jones–Irwin, 1979, pp. 53–4.
5. *Pension Task Force Report on Public Employee Retirement Systems.* Printed for the use of the Committee on Education and Labor, House of Representatives of the United States. Washington, D.C., 1978, p. 65.
6. *Ibid.,* p. 68.
7. *Ibid.,* pp. 147–48.
8. Gujarati, *op. cit.,* p. 15.
9. Louis Kohlmeier, *Conflict of Interest: State and Local Pension Fund Asset Management.* New York: Twentieth Century Fund, 1976, in *Pension Task Force Report,* p. 191.
10. *The Need For Overall Policy and Coordinated Management of Federal Retirement Systems.* Washington, D.C.: General Accounting Office, 12/29/78 (FPCD-78-49), p. 93.

CHAPTER 6

1. T. Harry Williams, *Huey Long.* New York: Bantam Books, Inc., 1970, p. 734.

2. Arther J. Altmeyer, *The Formative Years of Social Security*. Madison, Wisconsin: University of Wisconsin Press, 1966, p. 37.
3. Altmeyer, *op. cit.*, p. 50.
4. *Ibid.*, p. 228.
5. Theodore H. White, *The Making of the President, 1964*. New York: Atheneum Publishers, 1965, pp. 302–3.
6. Barry Goldwater, *The Coming Breakpoint*. New York: Macmillan Publishing Company, 1976, pp. 147–48.
7. Martha Derthick, *Policymaking for Social Security*. Washington, D.C.: The Brookings Institution, 1979, pp. 278–79.
8. *Ibid.*, p. 362.
9. *Ibid.*, p. 402n.
10. *Ibid.*, p. 408.
11. *Ibid.*, p. 411.
12. Stanford G. Ross, Commissioner of Social Security, *Testimony before the Subcommittee on Social Security of the House Ways and Means Committee, October 15, 1979*. Washington, D.C.: Reprint, Department of Health, Education, and Welfare, 1979, p. 1.
13. Ross, *Testimony,* September 28, 1979, p. 8.
14. *Ibid.*, p. 5.

CHAPTER 7

1. Barnet N. Berin, "Pensions U.S.A.—1977." In *Across The Board,* June 1978, p. 47.
2. "Employee Retirement Income Security Act of 1974: Comment on the Legislation—The Employee Benefits Industry." In *Pension & Welfare News,* November 1974, pp. 140–47.

CHAPTER 8

1. Louis Harris and Associates, Inc., *American Attitudes Toward Pensions and Retirement*. New York: Nationwide survey commissioned by Johnson & Higgins, 1979; vol. II, "Commentary," p. 4.
2. Elizabeth L. Meier and Cynthia C. Dittmar, "Varieties of Retirement Ages." Washington, D.C.: Unpublished working pa-

per for the President's Commission on Pension Policy (Revised) January 1980, pp. 107, 111.

CHAPTER 9

1. Catherine Drinker Bowen, *Francis Bacon, The Temper of a Man.* Boston: Little, Brown and Company, 1963, pp. 160–61.
2. Peter A. Dickinson, *The Complete Retirement Planning Book.* New York: E. P. Dutton & Co., 1976, p. 105.
3. *Ibid.,* p. 109.
4. *Ibid.,* p. 112.
5. *Ibid.,* p. 112.

Index

acquisitions and mergers, pension
plans in, 141–43
actuaries
accountability of, 65–66
assumptions by, 53–54
manipulation of, 61–62
client pressures on, 60–65
computer use by, 58–59
federal enrollment program for, 64
function of, 16, 52, 57
in management, 57–58
in marketing, 61
professional benefits for, 51–52
qualification requirements of, 51
for Social Security, 121, 122, 123–
24, 125–26
advertising, account executive role in,
59
Alliance Capital Management
Corporation, 48, 71
Altmeyer, Arthur J., 111, 112, 113,
115, 116, 117
American Express Company, 38–39
American Political Tradition, The
(Hofstadter), 35
American Society of Pension
Actuaries, 64
annuity
defined, 19
extra guarantees to, 24
origins of, 28–30
pure, 23
Arends, Verne J., 148
art, as investment, 192–93
for pension funds, 82–83
asset-management firms
fee schedules of, 71–72, 73
growth of, 69–70
pension funds under, 71

Babson, David, 77–78
Bacon, Sir Francis, 190–91

Ball, Robert M., 112, 123–24, 127,
128, 129, 134
Baltimore & Ohio Railroad Company,
39
Bankers Trust, 70
bank trust departments
fee schedules of, 71
pension fund management by, 68–
69, 70–71
Barksdale, Edgar, 81
Becker, George J., 26
Bendix Corporation, and Facet
pension plan, 63–64
Berin, Barnet N., 25, 53, 56–57, 61,
126, 146, 164
Bevan, David Crumley, 84
Bismarck, Otto von, 25, 45
Bludhorn, Charles G., 84–85
bonds, as retirement investment, 194–
95
Boston police strike (1919), 91
Boswell, James, 31, 32
Branch, C. B., 105
Bronner, David G., 101
Brooks, John, 65–66, 76
Brown Brothers Harriman &
Company, 71
Bundy, McGeorge, 74
Burr, Frank, 72

Cardwell, James B., 129
career-average pension formula, 21–22
Carnegie, Andrew, 40, 41–42
Carter, Jimmy, 129
Cary, Frank T., 105
Cary, William L., 77
Casdin, Jeffrey, 60
Casey, John, 81
Caterpillar Tractor, 62
Chandler, Alfred D., 36, 38
Charles II (King of England), 30
Chicago, public pension plans of, 88